FIRST 50
COUNTRY SONGS
YOU SHOULD PLAY ON THE PIANO

ISBN 978-1-4950-3589-0

HAL•LEONARD®
CORPORATION

7777 W. BLUEMOUND RD. P.O. BOX 13819 MILWAUKEE, WI 53213

Visit Hal Leonard Online at
www.halleonard.com

CONTENTS

BEHIND CLOSED DOORS

Words and Music by
KENNY O'DELL

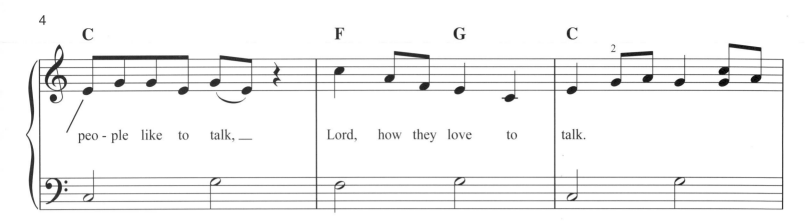

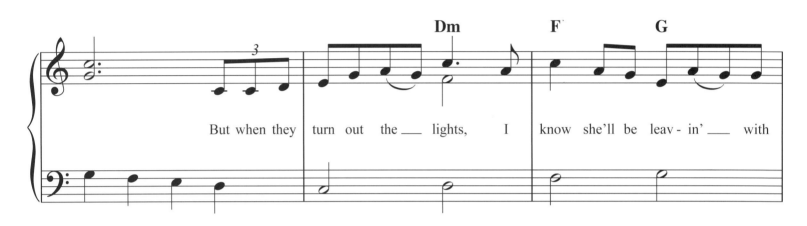

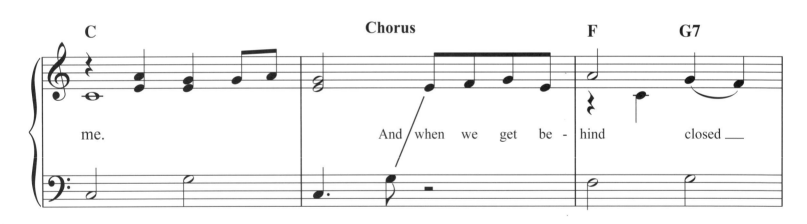

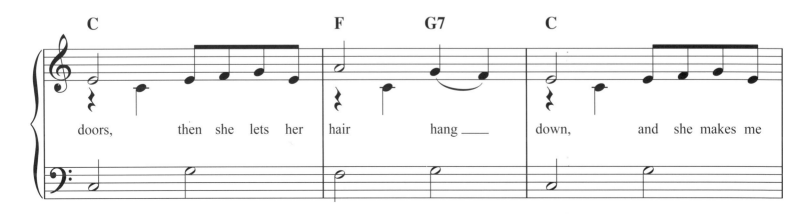

glad   I'm ___ a   man; ___   oh,   no   one   knows   what

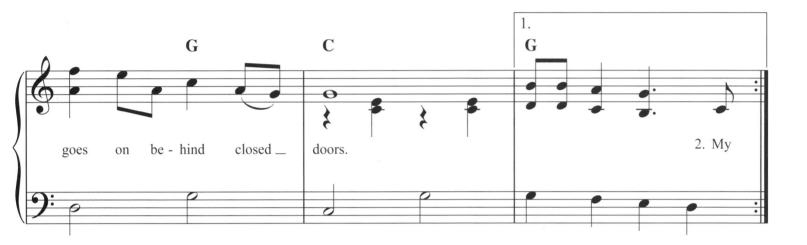

goes   on   be - hind   closed __   doors.   2. My

Be - hind   closed ___   doors. ___   *rit.*

Additional Lyrics

2. My baby makes me smile, Lord, don't she make me smile.
   She's never far away or too tired to say I want you.
   She's always a lady, just like a lady should be.
   But when they turn out the lights, she's still a baby to me.
   Chorus

ALL MY EX'S LIVE IN TEXAS

Words and Music by LYNDIA J. SHAFER
and SANGER D. SHAFER

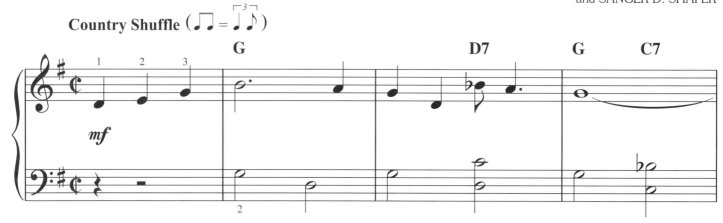

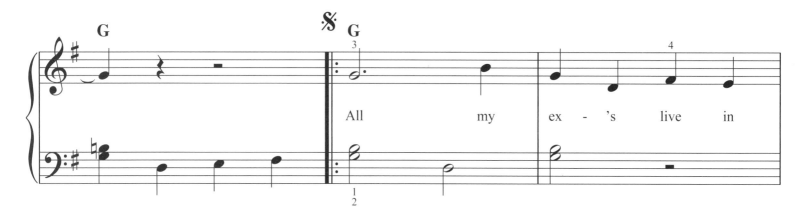

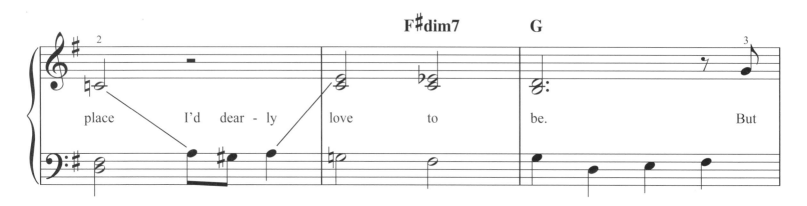

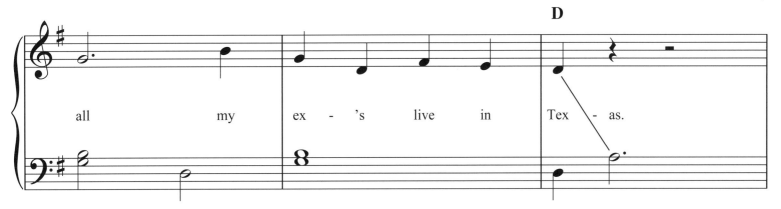

all   my   ex - 's   live   in   Tex - as.

To Coda ⊕

{ (1., 2.) And that's   why   I   hang   my   hat ____   in Ten - nes -
{ (D.S.) There -

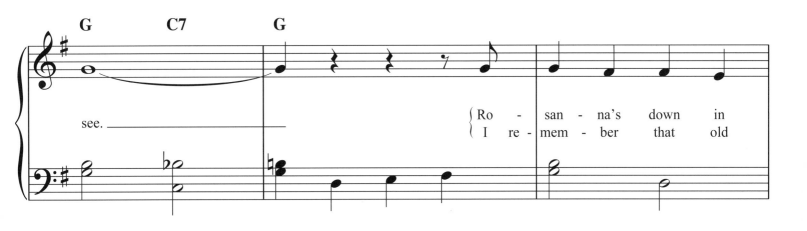

see. ____

{ Ro - san - na's   down   in
{ I re - mem - ber   that   old

Tex - ar - ka - na;   want - ed me to push her broom.   And
Fri - o Riv - er   where I learned to ____ swim.   And it

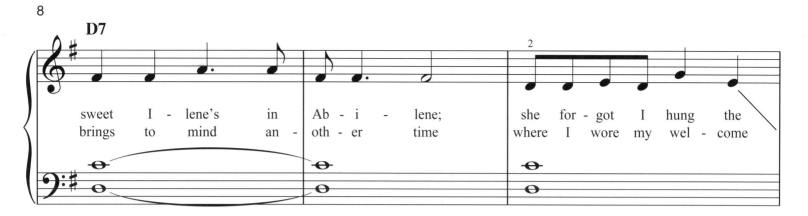

sweet I - lene's in Ab - i - lene;
brings to mind an - oth - er time

she for - got I hung the
where I wore my wel - come

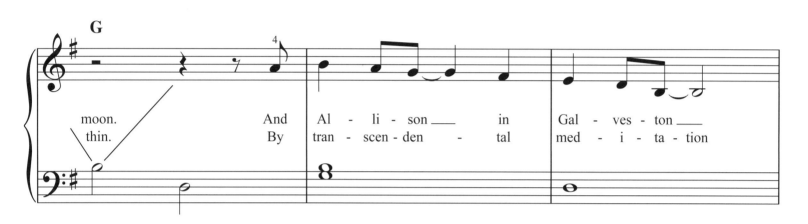

moon. And Al - li - son ___ in
thin. By tran - scen - den - tal

Gal - ves - ton ___
med - i - ta - tion

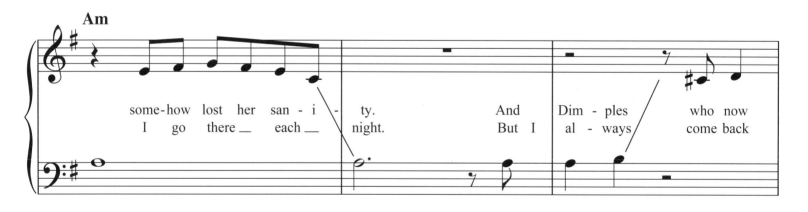

some-how lost her san - i - ty.
I go there ___ each ___ night.

And Dim - ples who now
But I al - ways come back

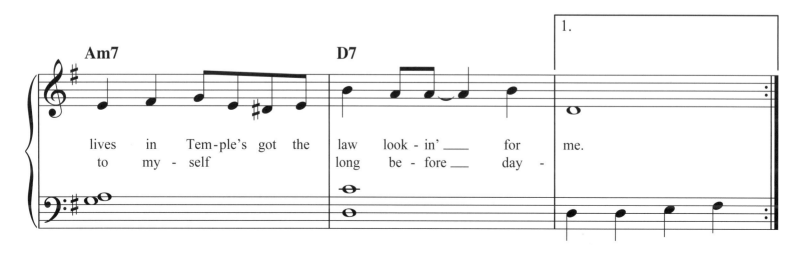

lives in Tem - ple's got the
to my - self

law look - in' ___ for me.
long be - fore ___ day -

D.S. al Coda

light.

CODA

G

fore, I re - side ___ in Ten - nes - see. ___

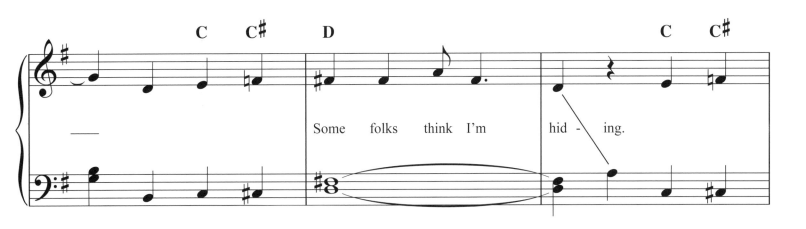

C **C♯** **D** **C** **C♯**

___ Some folks think I'm hid - ing.

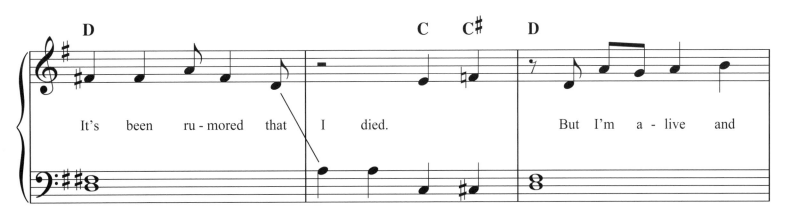

D **C** **C♯** **D**

It's been ru - mored that I died. But I'm a - live and

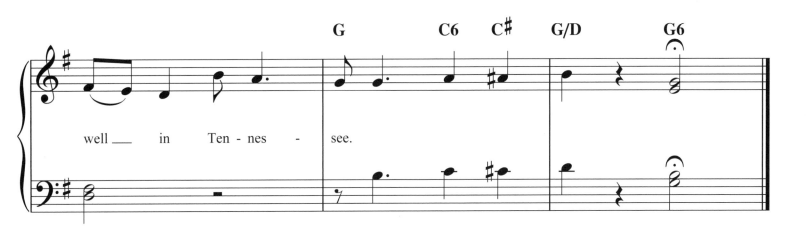

G **C6** **C♯** **G/D** **G6**

well ___ in Ten - nes - see.

ALWAYS ON MY MIND

Words and Music by WAYNE THOMPSON,
MARK JAMES and JOHNNY CHRISTOPHER

Moderately slow

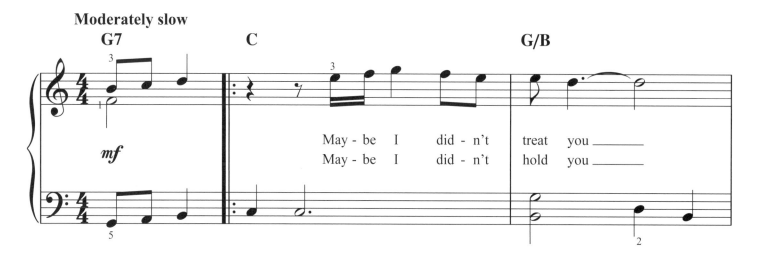

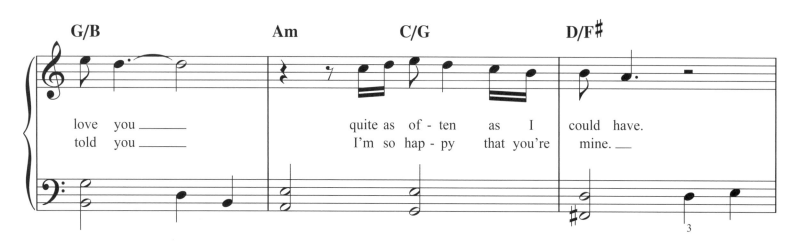

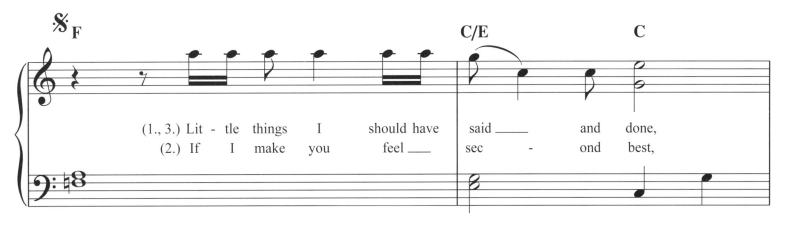

(1., 3.) Lit - tle things I should have said _____ and done,
(2.) If I make you feel _____ sec - ond best,

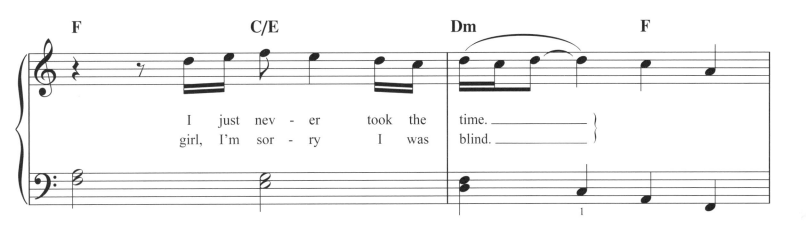

I just nev - er took the time. _____
girl, I'm sor - ry I was blind. _____

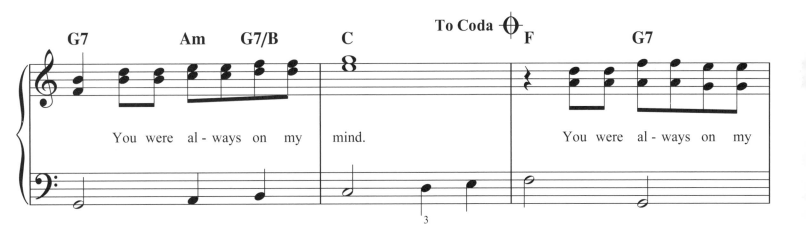

You were al - ways on my mind.

You were al - ways on my

mind.

mind.

Tell _____ me,

tell me that your sweet love ___ has-n't died. ___ Give ___

me, give me one more chance to keep you sat - is - fied, ___ sat - is -

fied. You are al - ways on my

mind. ___ You are al - ways on my mind.

BLUE EYES CRYING IN THE RAIN

Words and Music by
FRED ROSE

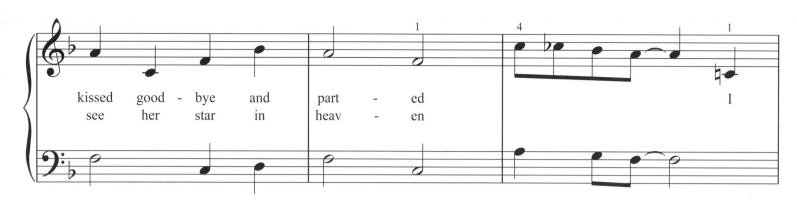

kissed good - bye and part - ed
see her star in heav - en

I

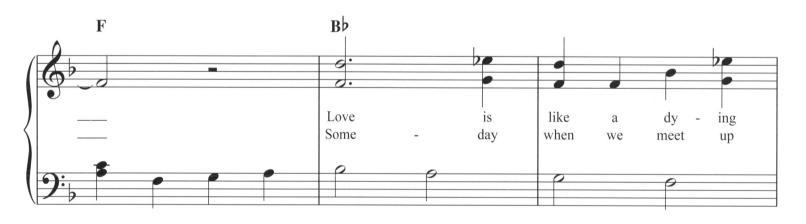

C7   F   Bb

knew we'd nev - er meet a - gain.
blue eyes cry - ing in the rain.

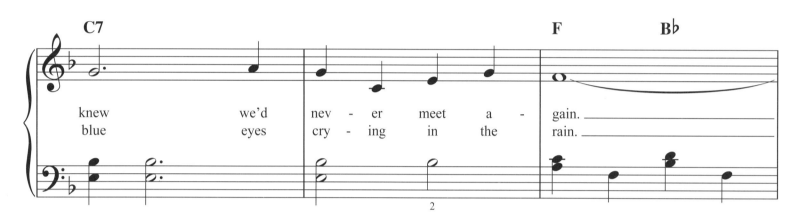

F   Bb

Love is like a dy - ing
Some - day when we meet up

F

em - ber on - ly
yon - der we'll stroll

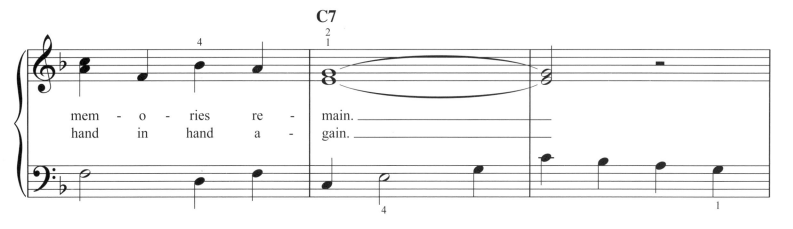

C7

mem - o - ries re - main. _____
hand in hand a - gain. _____

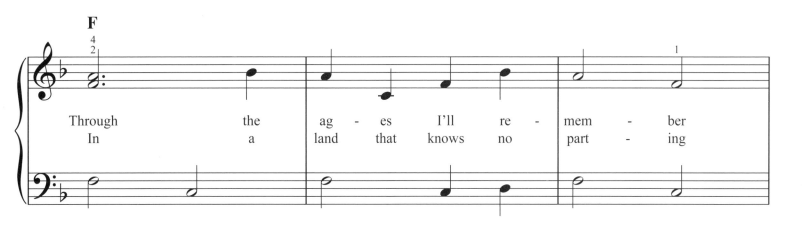

F

Through the ag - es I'll re - mem - ber
In a land that knows no part - ing

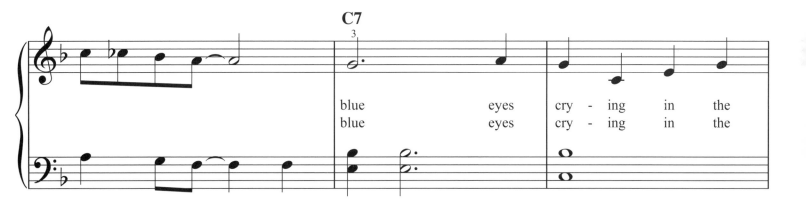

C7

blue eyes cry - ing in the
blue eyes cry - ing in the

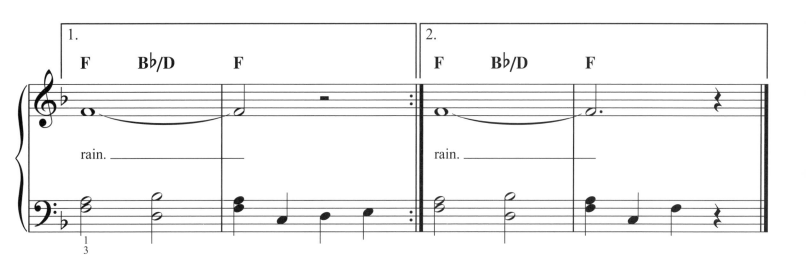

1.

F   **B♭/D**   **F**

rain. _____

2.

F   **B♭/D**   **F**

rain. _____

BLUE BAYOU

Words and Music by ROY ORBISON
and JOE MELSON

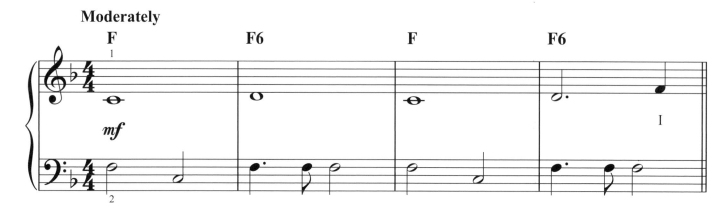

feel so bad, __ I've got a wor - ried mind; I'm so lone - some
Go to see __ my ba - by a - gain and to be with

all the time, since I left my ba - by be - hind __ on __
some of my friends; may - be I'd be hap - py then __ on __

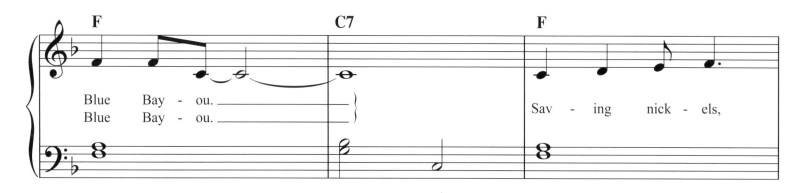

Blue Bay - ou. _____
Blue Bay - ou. _____

Sav - ing nick - els,

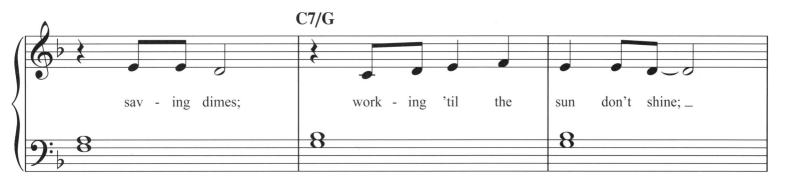

C7/G

sav - ing dimes;   work - ing 'til the   sun don't shine; __

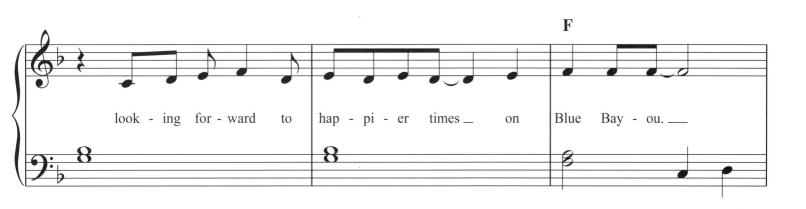

F

look - ing for - ward to   hap - pi - er times __ on   Blue Bay - ou. __

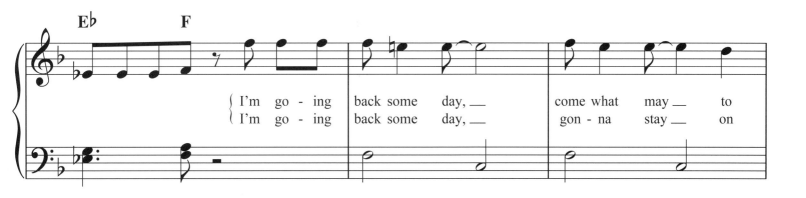

E♭   **F**

I'm go - ing | back some day, __   come what may __ to
I'm go - ing | back some day, __   gon - na stay __ on

C7

Blue Bay - ou, _____   where you   sleep all day __ and the
Blue Bay - ou, _____   where the   folks are fine __ and the

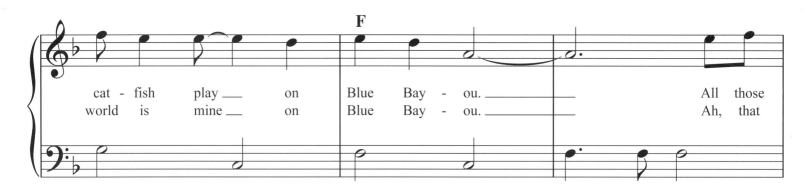

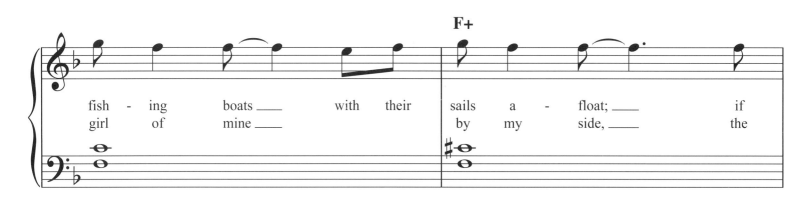

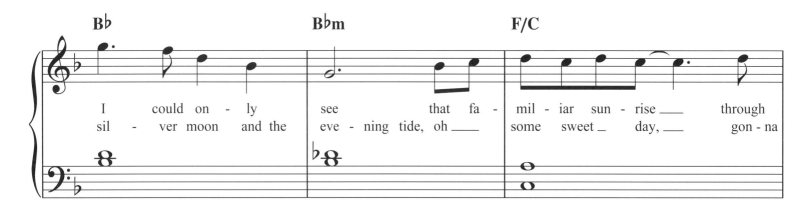

hurt - in' in - side. _____ I'll nev - er be blue; __ my

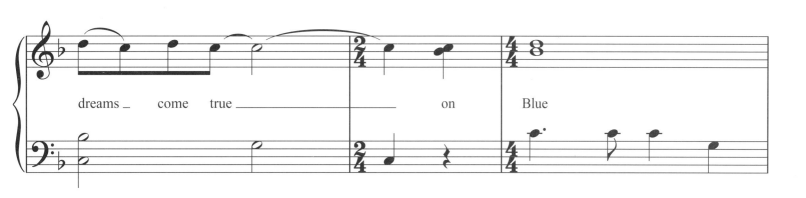

dreams _ come true _____ on Blue

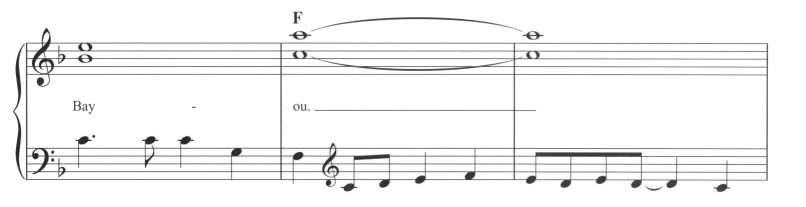

Bay - ou. _____

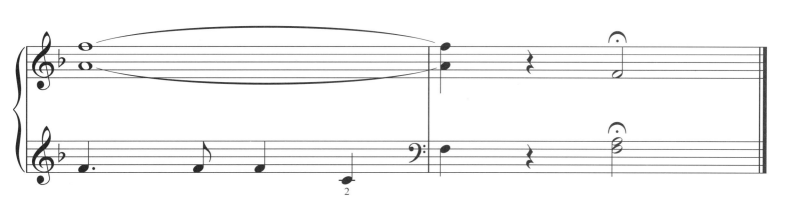

BORN TO LOSE

Words and Music by
TED DAFFAN

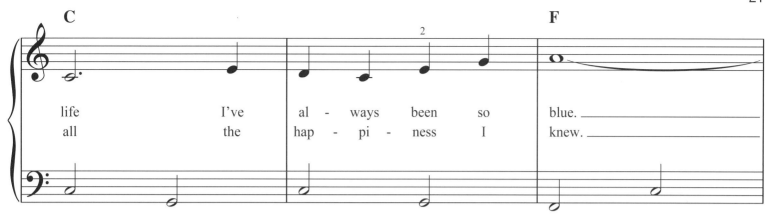

C ... **F**

life   I've   al - ways been so   blue. _____

all   the   hap - pi - ness I   knew. _____

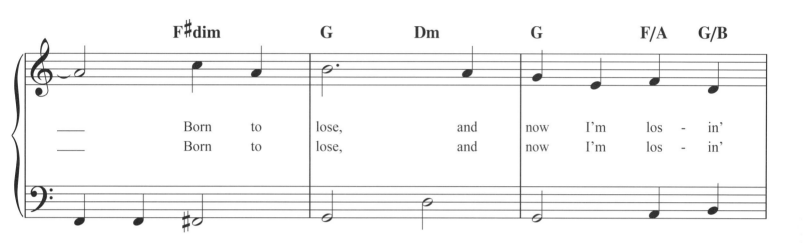

F#dim   **G**   **Dm**   **G**   **F/A**   **G/B**

____ Born to lose,   and now I'm los - in'

____ Born to lose,   and now I'm los - in'

C   **E♭dim7**   **G**   **Am**   **G/B**   **C**

you.   Born to lose,   it

you.   There's no use   to

F   **G**   **C**

seems so hard to bear, _____ how I

dream of hap - pi - ness, _____ all I

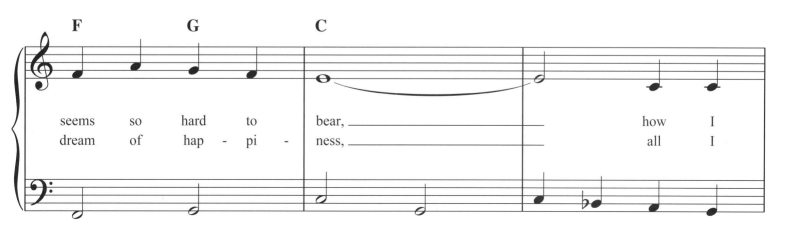

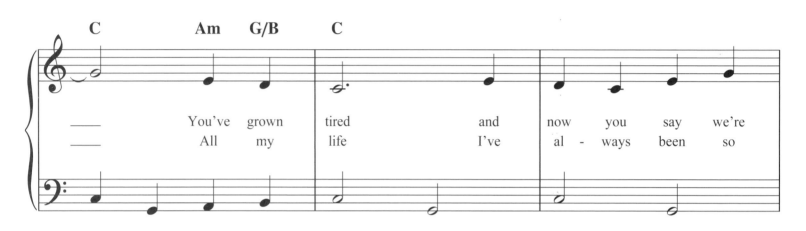

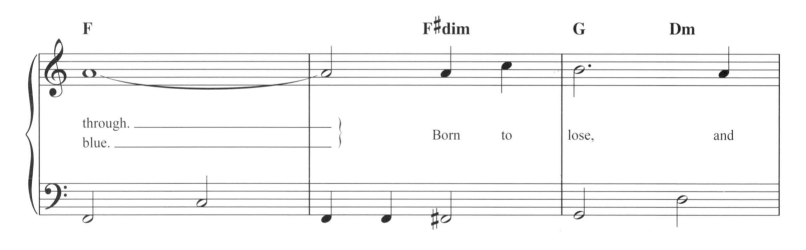

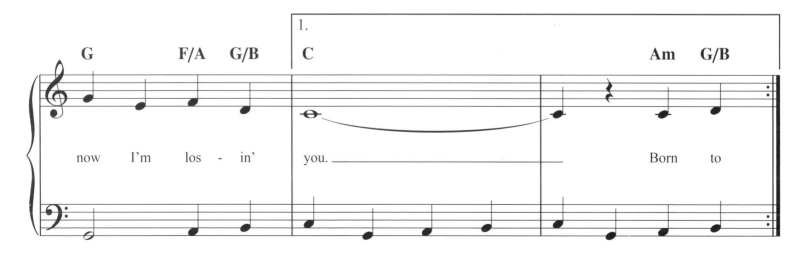

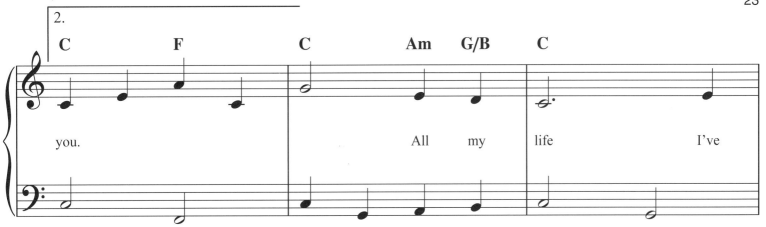

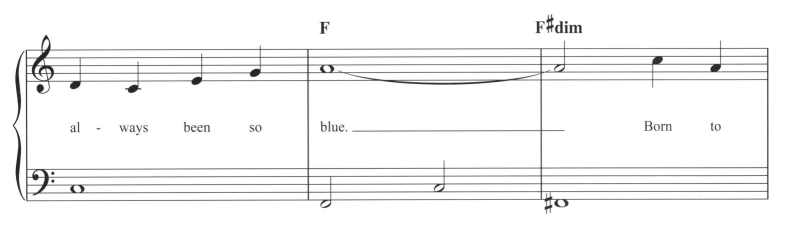

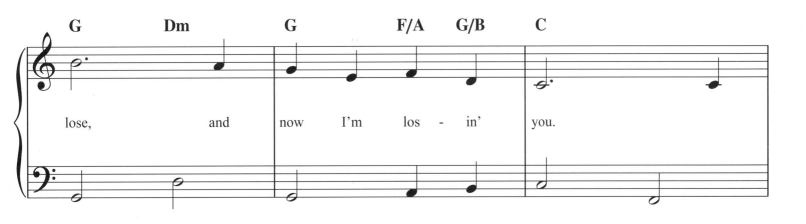

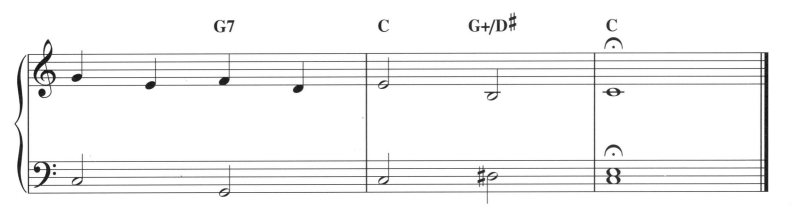

COULD I HAVE THIS DANCE

from URBAN COWBOY

Words and Music by WAYLAND HOLYFIELD
and BOB HOUSE

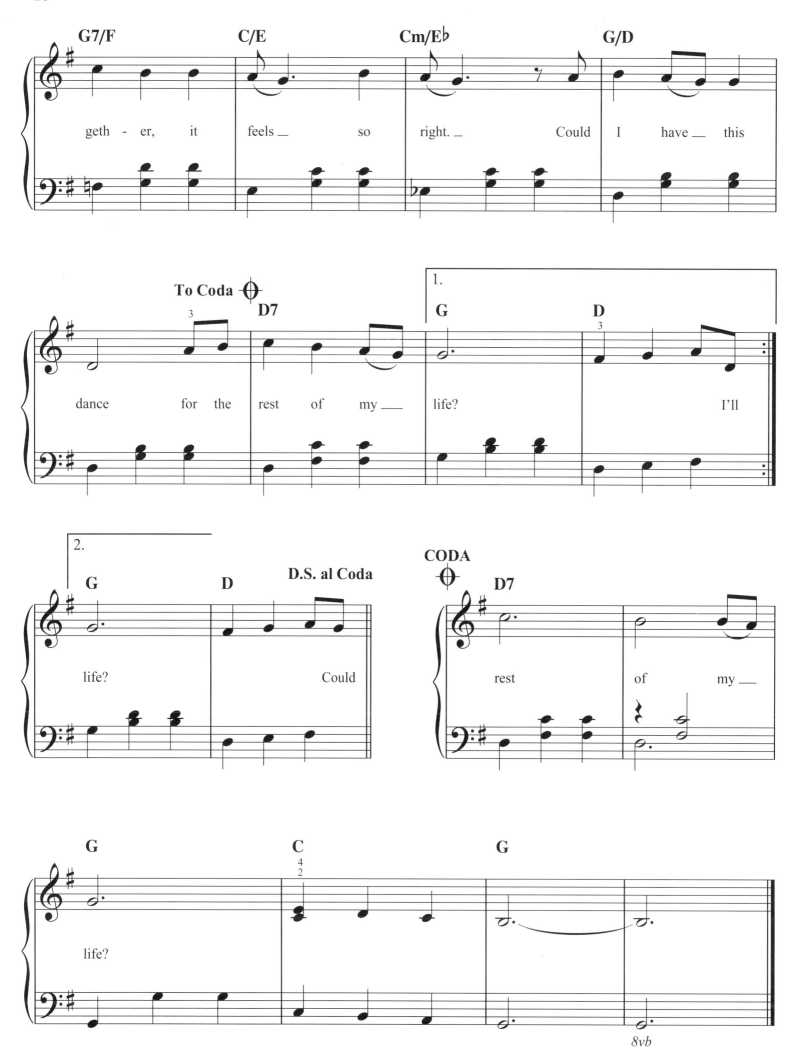

CRAZY

Words and Music by
WILLIE NELSON

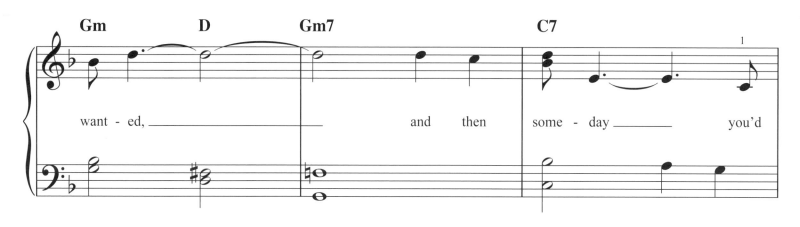

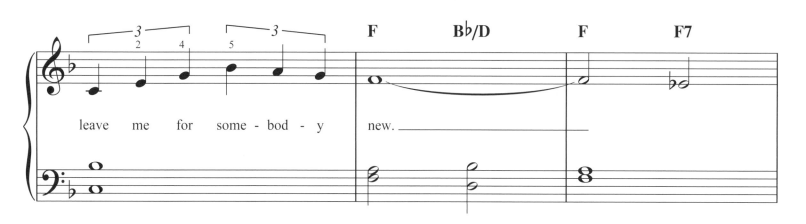

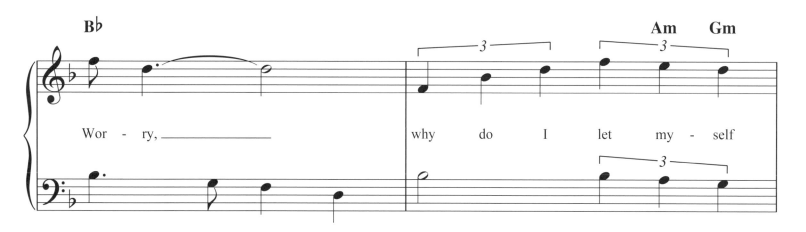

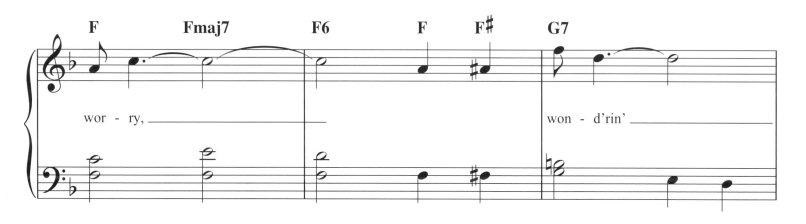

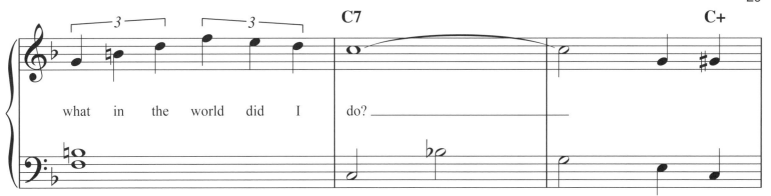

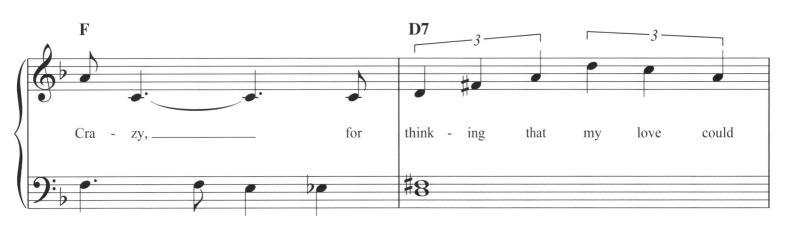

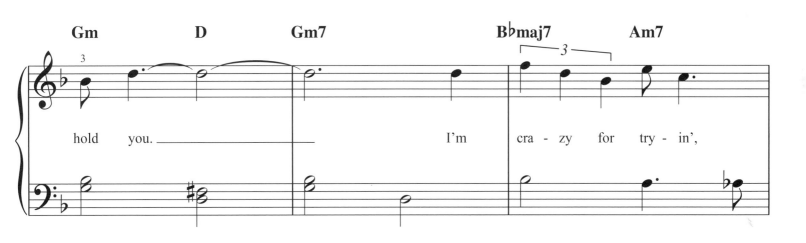

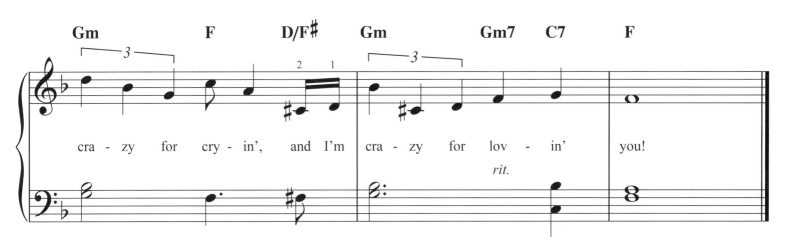

THE DANCE

Words and Music by
TONY ARATA

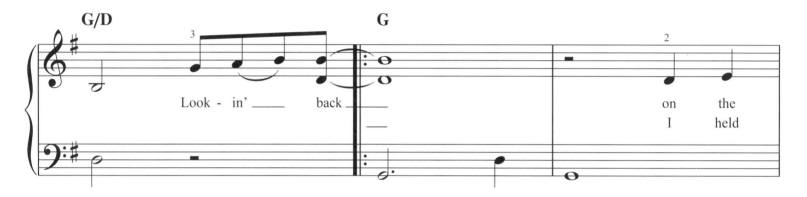

Look - in' _____ back _____ on the
I held

mem - 'ry of _____ the dance we shared _____
ev - 'ry - thing _____ for a mo - ment. _____

with all the stars a - bove, ____ for a
Was - n't I the king? ____ If I'd

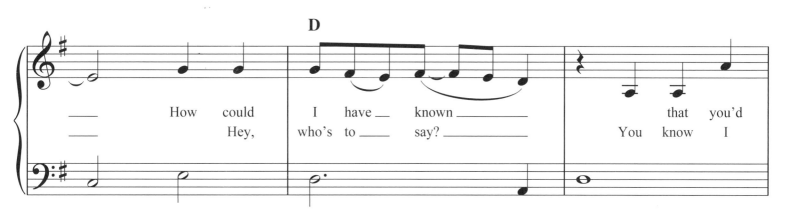

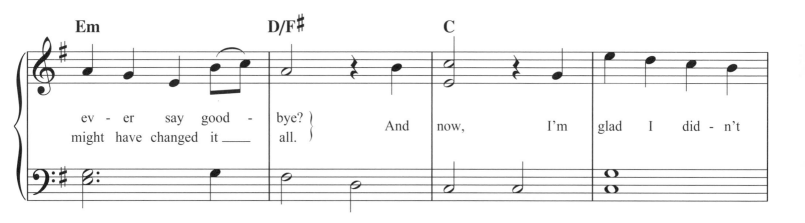

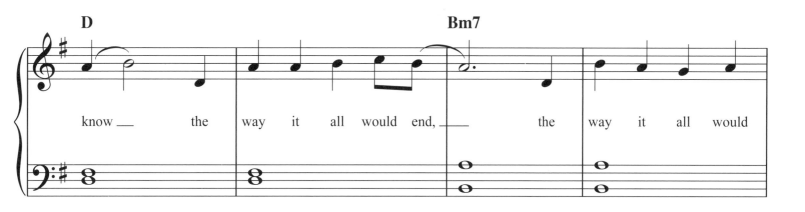

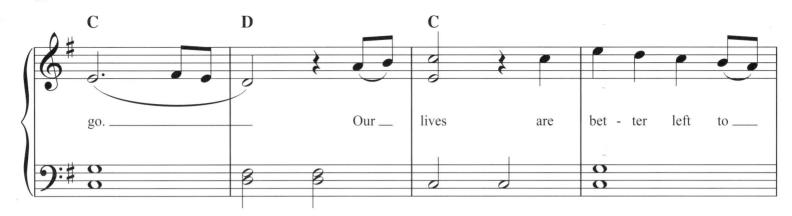

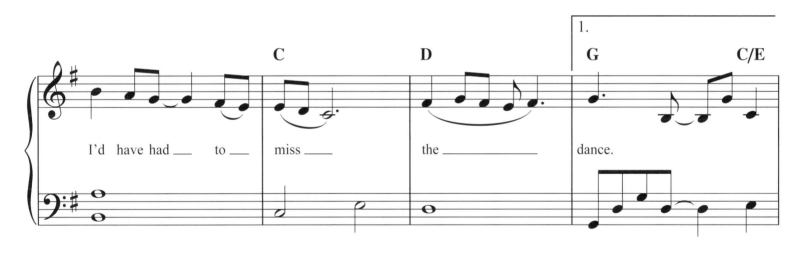

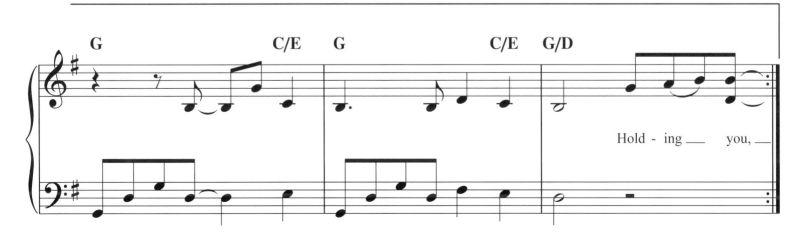

dance. Yes, my life, it's bet - ter left to ___

chance. ___ I could have missed ___ the pain, _____ but

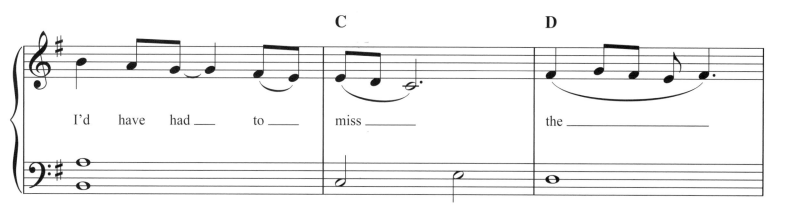

I'd have had ___ to ___ miss _____ the _____

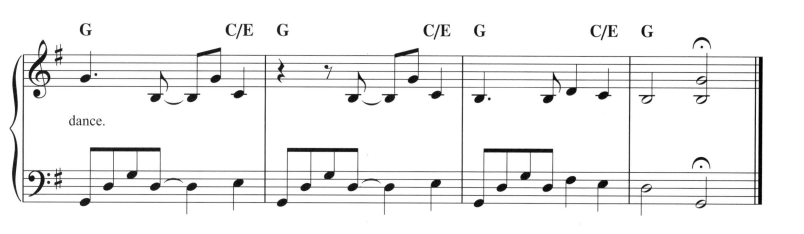

dance.

DON'T IT MAKE MY
BROWN EYES BLUE

Words and Music by
RICHARD LEIGH

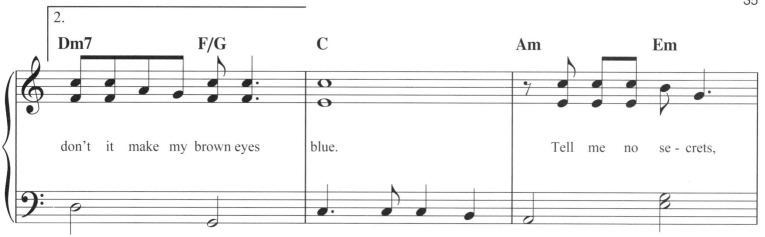

don't it make my brown eyes blue. Tell me no se - crets,

tell me some lies, give me no rea - sons, __ give me

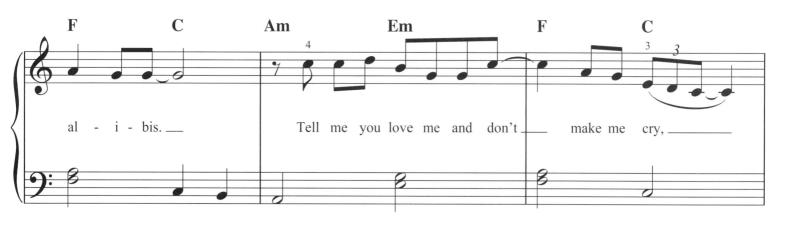

al - i - bis. __ Tell me you love me and don't __ make me cry, __

D.S. al Coda

say an - y - thing but don't say good - bye. __

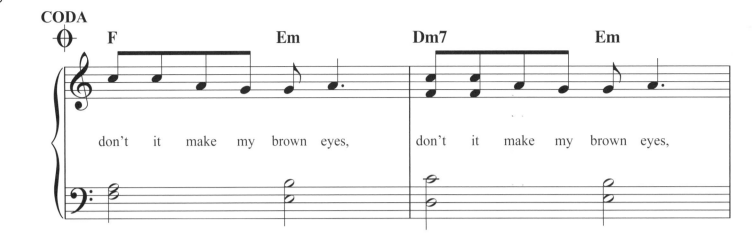

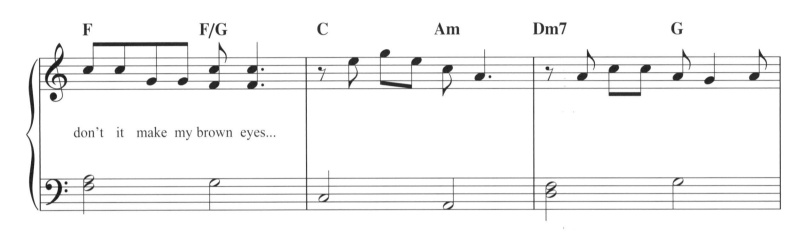

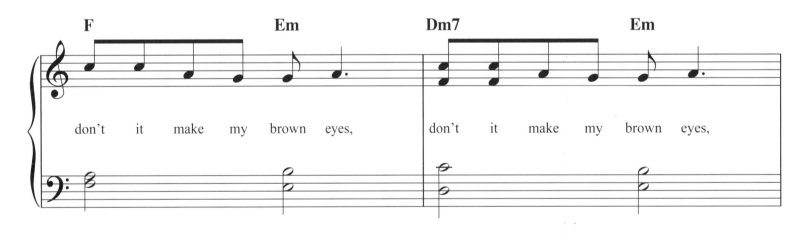

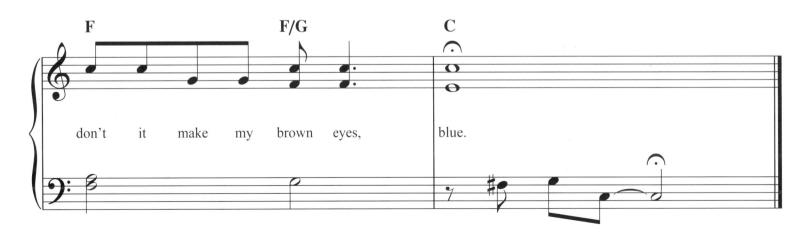

EL PASO

Words and Music by
MARTY ROBBINS

Moderately

Out in the | West Tex - as | town of El
Night - time would | find me in | Ro - sa's Can -

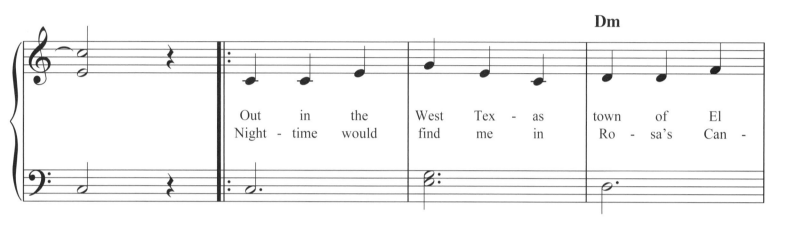

Pa - so, | I fell in | love with a | Mex - i - can
ti - na. | Mu - sic would | play and Fe - | li - na would

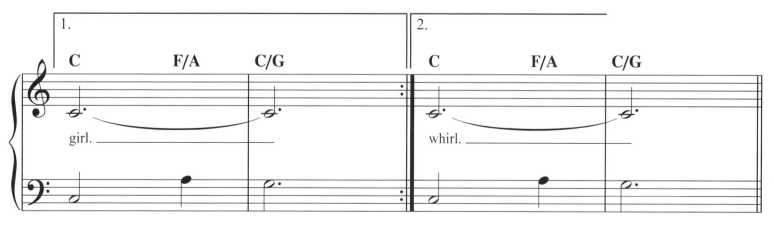

1.
girl.

2.
whirl.

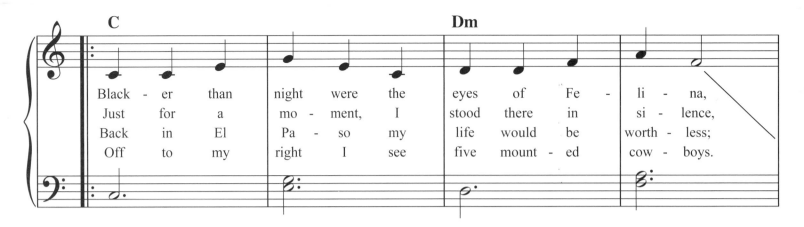

Black - er than night were the eyes of Fe - li - na,
Just for a mo - ment, I stood there in si - lence,
Back in El Pa - so my life would be worth - less;
Off to my right I see five mount - ed cow - boys.

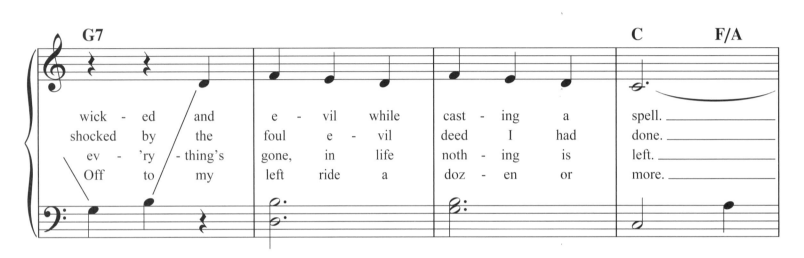

wick - ed and e - vil while cast - ing a spell.
shocked by the foul e - vil deed I had done.
ev - 'ry - thing's gone, in life noth - ing is left.
Off to my left ride a doz - en or more.

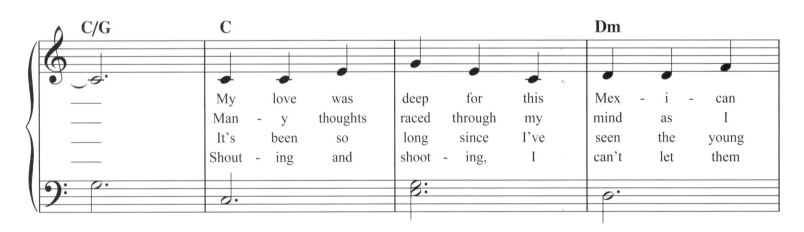

My love was deep for this Mex - i - can
Man - y thoughts raced through my mind as I
It's been so long since I've seen the young
Shout - ing and shoot - ing, I can't let them

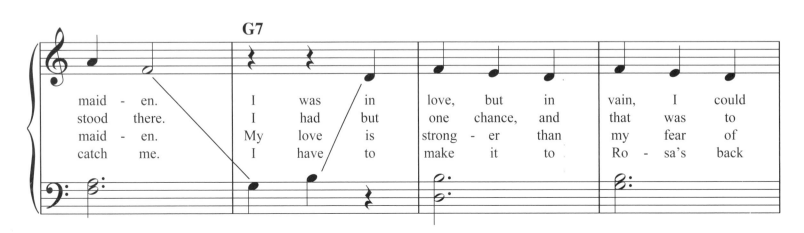

maid - en. I was in love, but in vain, I could
stood there. I had but one chance, and that was to
maid - en. My love is strong - er than my fear of
catch me. I have to make it to Ro - sa's back

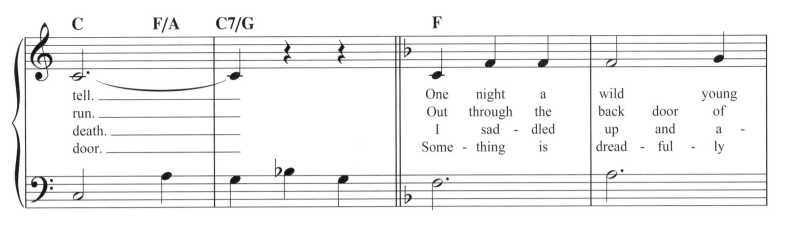

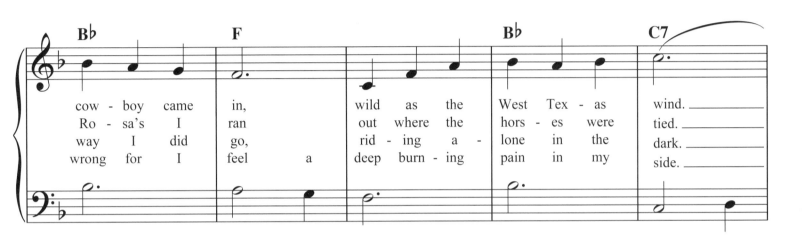

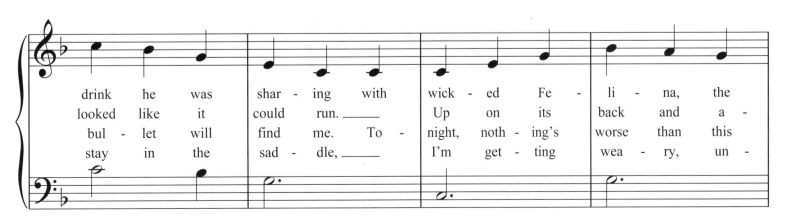

girl that I loved. _____ So, in an - ger, I
way I did ride _____ just as fast as I
pain in my heart. _____ And at last, here I
a - ble to ride. _____ But my love for Fe -

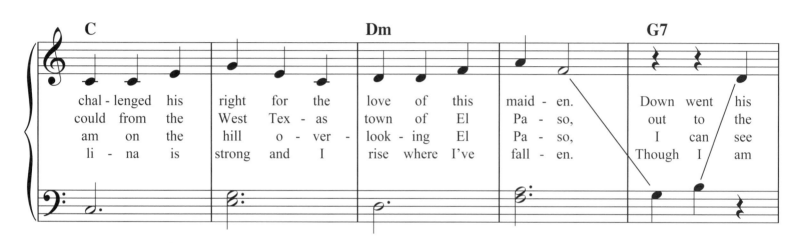

chal - lenged his right for the love of this maid - en. Down went his
could from the West Tex - as town of El Pa - so, out to the
am on the hill o - ver - look - ing El Pa - so, I can see
li - na is strong and I rise where I've fall - en. Though I am

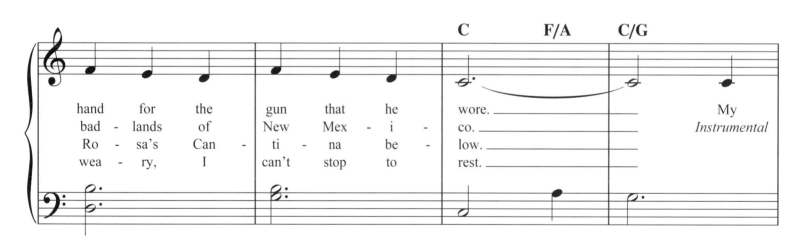

hand for the gun that he wore. _____ My
bad - lands of New Mex - i - co. _____ *Instrumental*
Ro - sa's Can - ti - na be - low. _____
wea - ry, I can't stop to rest. _____

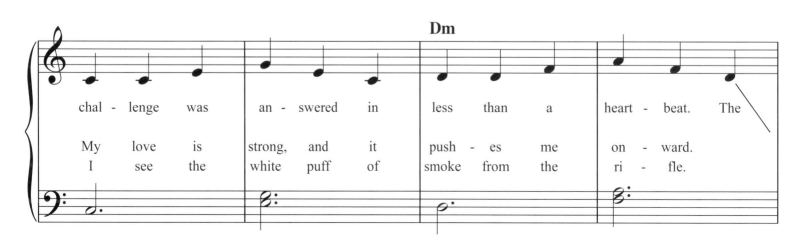

chal - lenge was an - swered in less than a heart - beat. The
My love is strong, and it push - es me on - ward.
I see the white puff of smoke from the ri - fle.

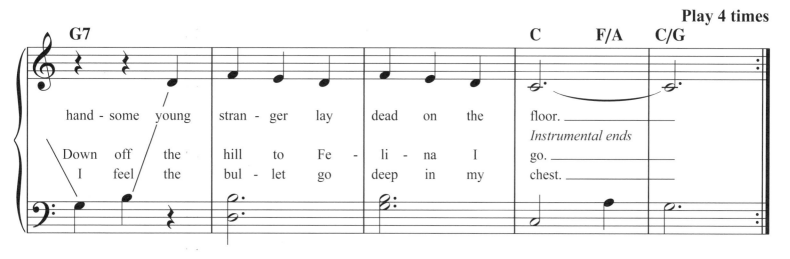

G7   C   F/A   C/G

hand - some young stran - ger lay dead on the floor. _____
Instrumental ends
Down off the hill to Fe - li - na I go. _____
I feel the bul - let go deep in my chest. _____

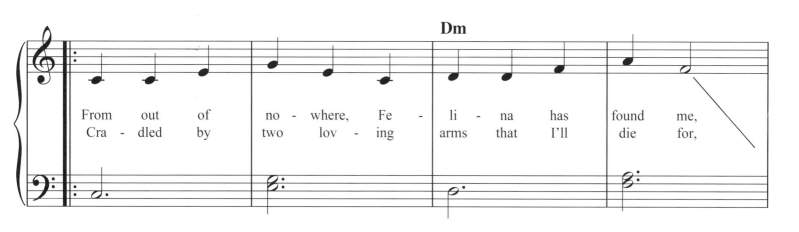

Dm

From out of no - where, Fe - li - na has found me,
Cra - dled by two lov - ing arms that I'll die for,

G7   1.
      C   F/A   C/G

kiss - ing my cheek as she kneels by my side. _____
one lit - tle kiss, then, Fe - li - na, good

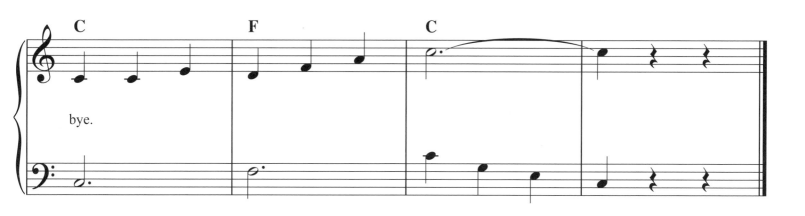

C   F   C

bye.

GENTLE ON MY MIND

Words and Music by
JOHN HARTFORD

Moderately

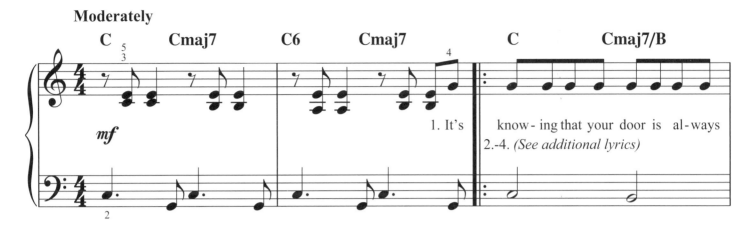

1. It's know-ing that your door is al-ways
2.-4. *(See additional lyrics)*

o - pen and your path is free to walk, that

makes me tend to leave my sleep-ing bag rolled up and stashed be - hind your

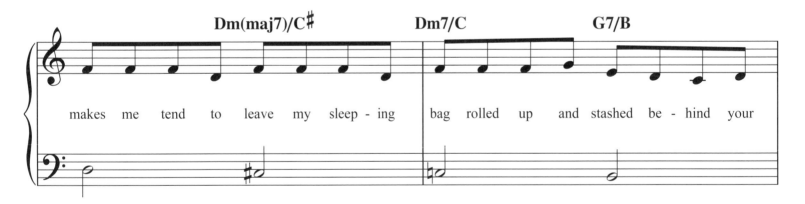

couch. And it's know-ing I'm not shack-led by for-

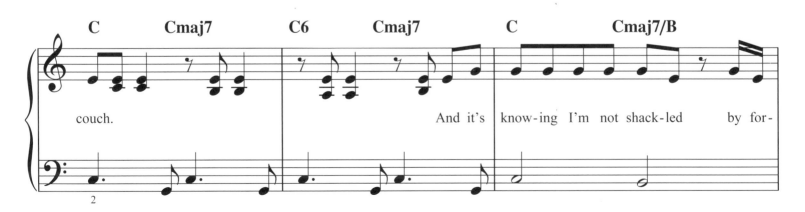

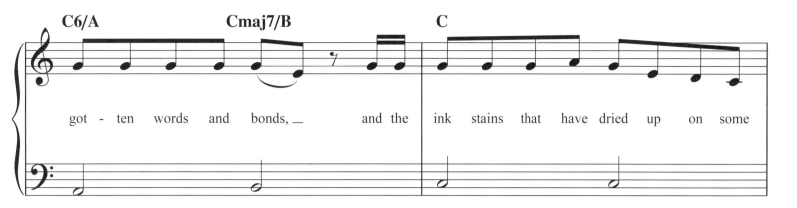

got - ten words and bonds, ___ and the ink stains that have dried up on some

line, that keeps you in the back-roads by the

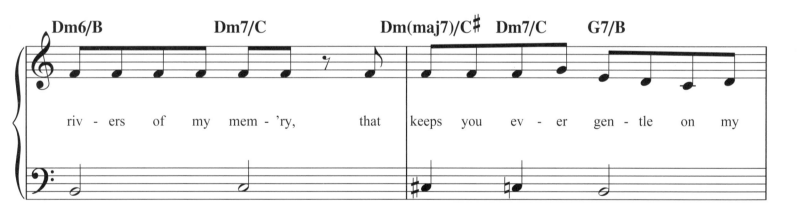

riv - ers of my mem - 'ry, that keeps you ev - er gen - tle on my

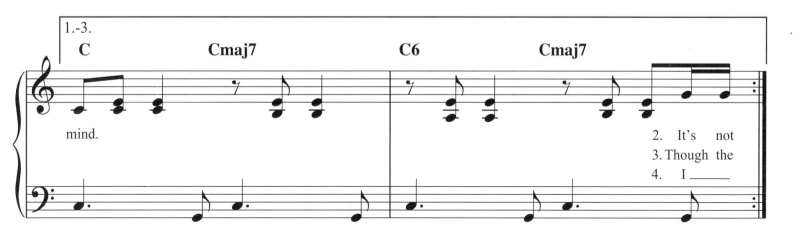

mind.

2. It's not
3. Though the
4. I ____

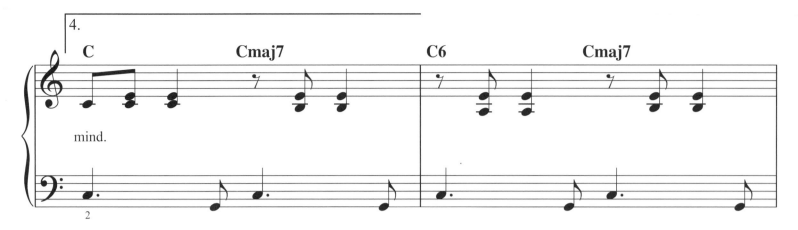

Additional Lyrics

2. It's not clinging to the rocks and ivy planted on their columns now that binds me,
   Or something that somebody said because they thought we fit together walkin'.
   It's just knowing that the world will not be cursing or forgiving when I walk along some
      railroad track and find
   That you're moving on the backroads by the rivers of my memory, and for hours you're just
      gentle on my mind.

3. Though the wheat fields and the clotheslines and junkyards and the highways come between us,
   And some other woman crying to her mother 'cause she turned away and I was gone.
   I still run in silence, tears of joy might stain my face and summer sun might burn me 'til I'm blind.
   But not to where I cannot see you walkin' on the backroads by the rivers flowing gentle on my mind.

4. I dip my cup of soup back from the gurglin' cracklin' caldron in some train yard,
   My beard, a rough'ning coal pile and a dirty hat pulled low across my face.
   Through cupped hands 'round a tin can I pretend I hold you to my breast and find
   That you're waving from the backroads by the rivers of my memory ever smilin' ever
      gentle on my mind.

FOLSOM PRISON BLUES

Words and Music by
JOHN R. CASH

Moderately

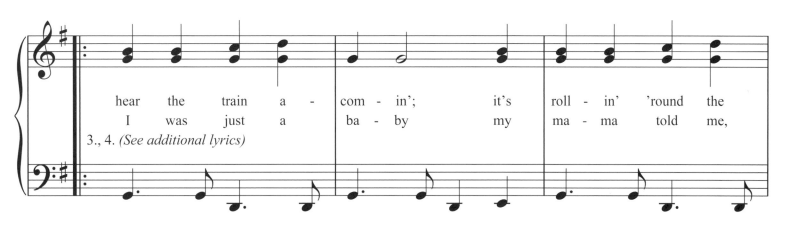

hear the train a - com - in'; it's roll - in' 'round the
I was just a ba - by my ma - ma told me,
3., 4. *(See additional lyrics)*

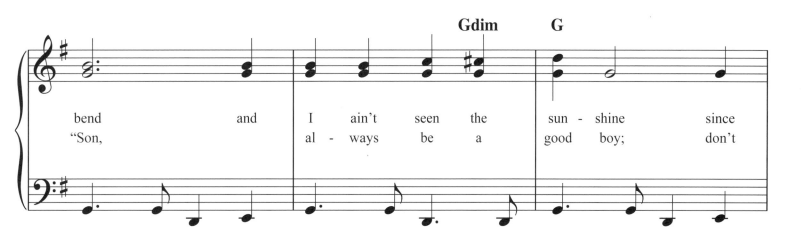

bend and I ain't seen the sun - shine since
"Son, al - ways be a good boy; don't

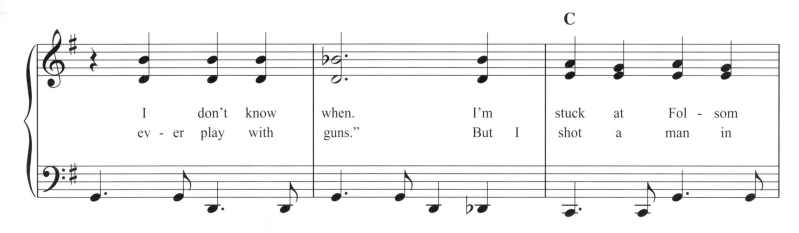

I   don't know   when.   I'm   stuck at   Fol - som
ev - er play with   guns."   But I   shot   a   man   in

Pri - son   and time keeps   drag - gin'
Re - no   just   to   watch   him

on. _____
die. _____

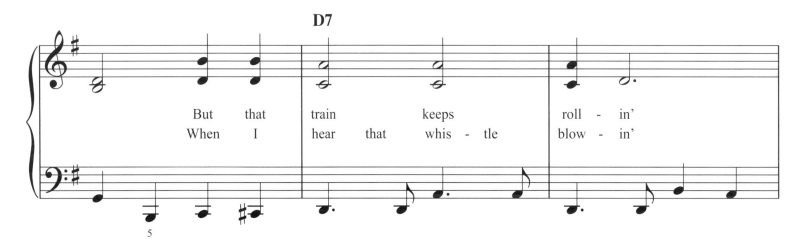

But   that   train   keeps   roll - in'
When I   hear that   whis - tle   blow - in'

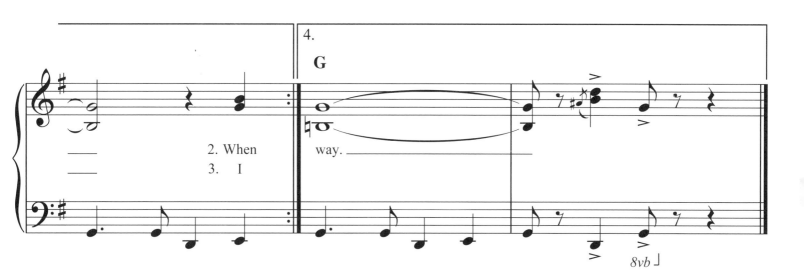

Additional Lyrics

3. I bet there's rich folks eatin' in a fancy dining car.
   They're prob'ly drinkin' coffee and smokin' big cigars.
   But I know I had it comin', I know I can't be free,
   But those people keep a-movin', and that's what tortures me.

4. Well, if they freed me from this prison, if that railroad train was mine,
   I bet I'd move on over a little farther down the line.
   Far from Folsom Prison, that's where I want to stay,
   And I'd let that lonesome whistle blow my blues away.

FOREVER AND EVER, AMEN

Words and Music by PAUL OVERSTREET
and DON SCHLITZ

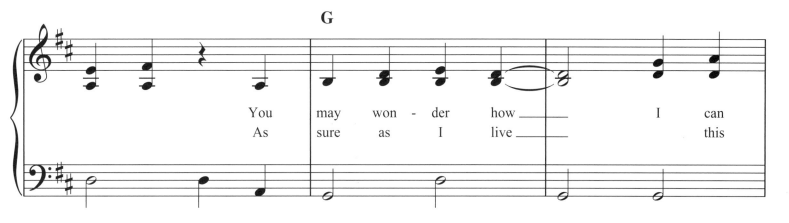

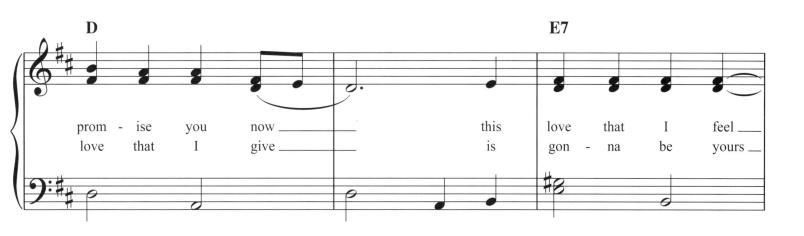

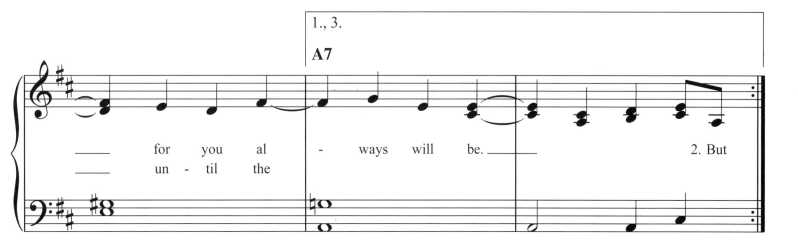

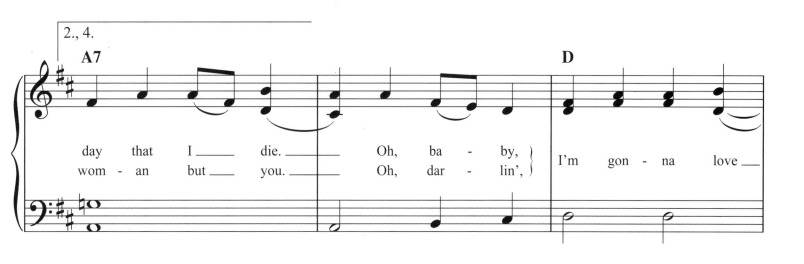

50

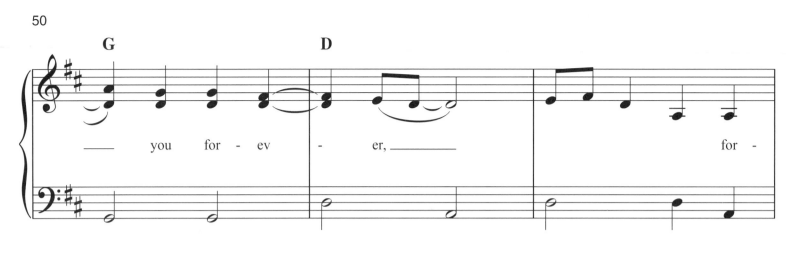

you for - ev - er, _____ for -

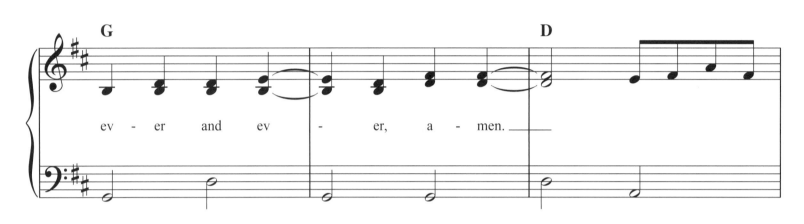

ev - er and ev - er, a - men. ____

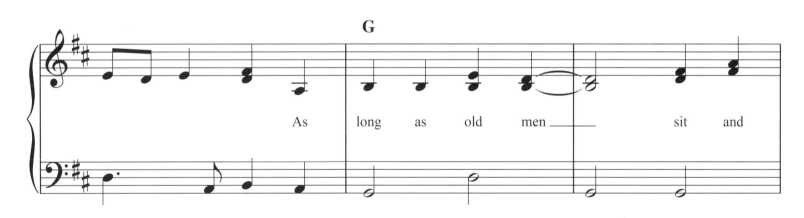

As long as old men ____ sit and

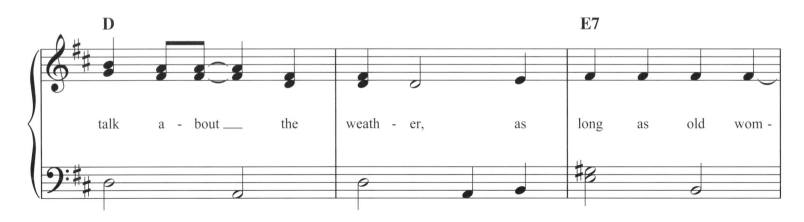

talk a - bout ___ the weath - er, as long as old wom -

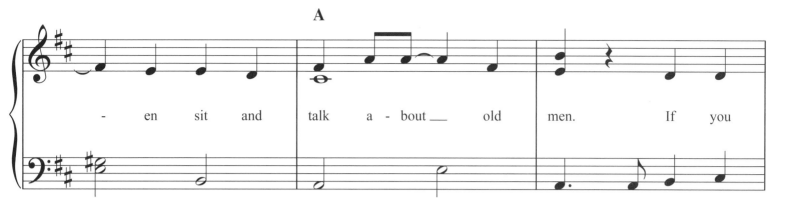

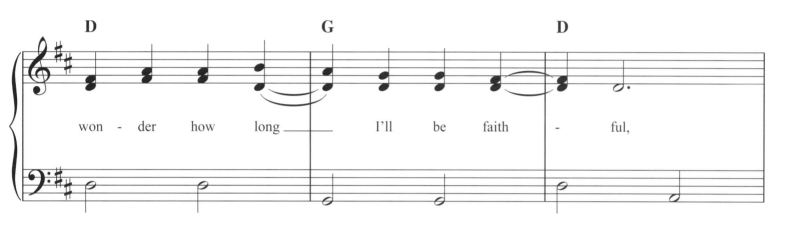

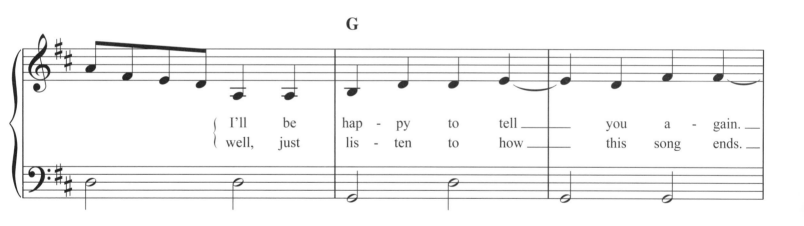

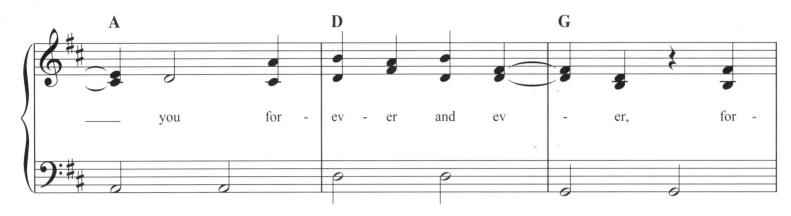

you for - ev - er and ev - er, for -

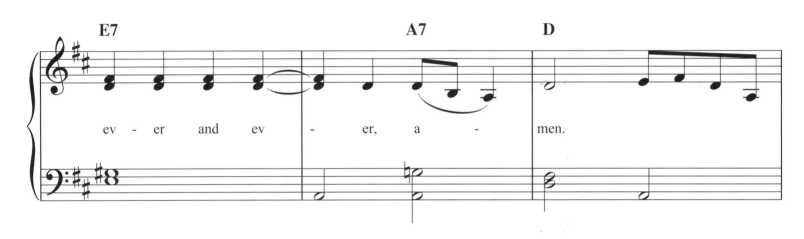

ev - er and ev - er, a - men.

To Coda ⊕

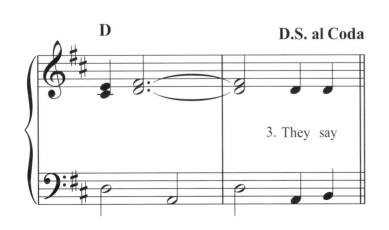

D.S. al Coda

3. They say

CODA ⊕

I'm gon - na love ___ you for -

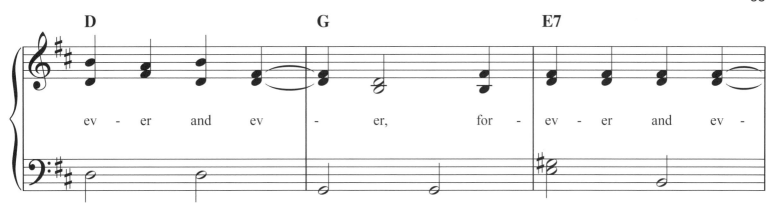

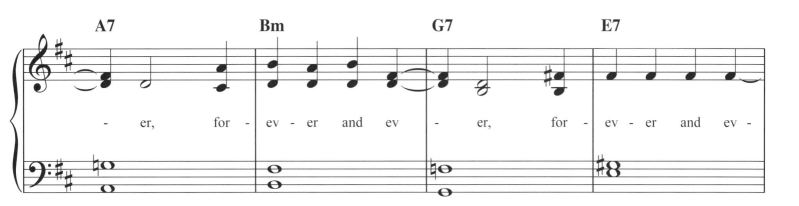

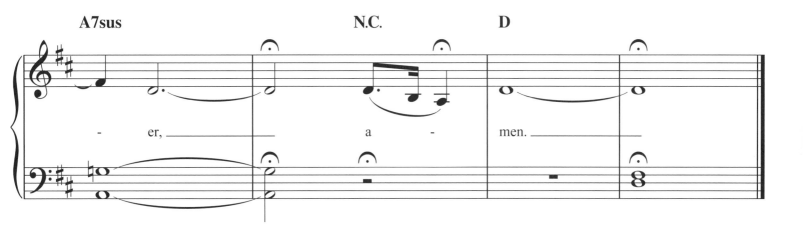

Additional Lyrics

3. They say time takes its toll on a body,
   Makes a young girl's brown hair turn gray.
   Well, honey, I don't care,
   I ain't in love with your hair,
   And if it all fell out, well, I'd love you anyway.

4. They say time can play tricks on a memory,
   Make people forget things they knew.
   Well, it's easy to see
   It's happenin' to me.
   I've already forgotten every woman but you.

FRIENDS IN LOW PLACES

Words and Music by DEWAYNE BLACKWELL
and EARL BUD LEE

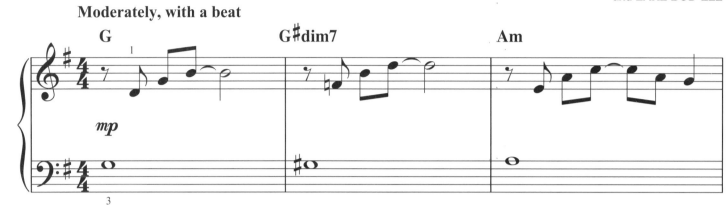

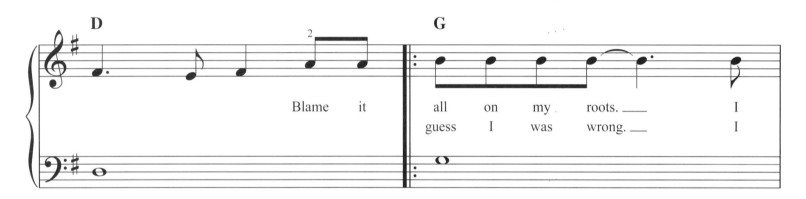

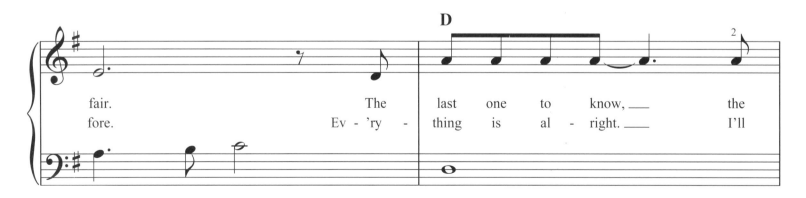

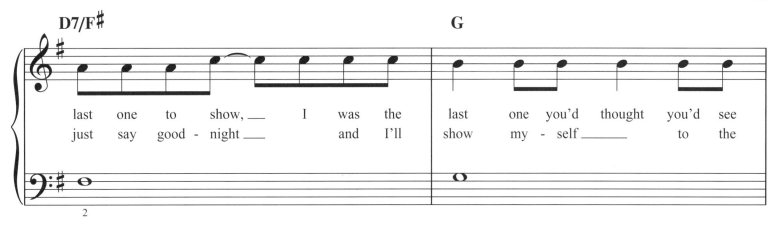

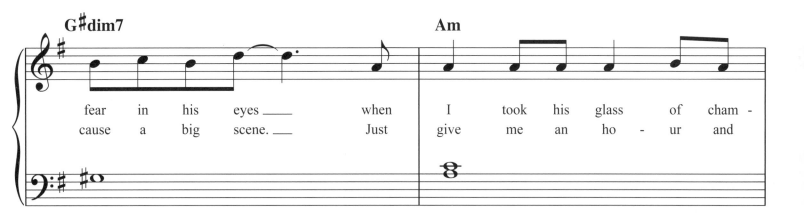

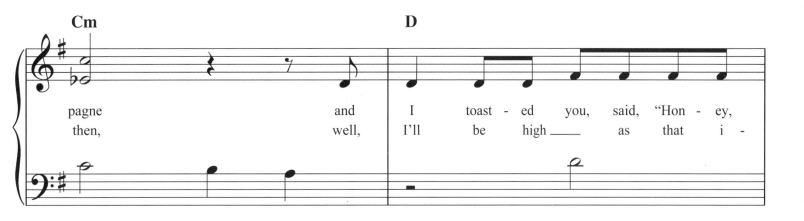

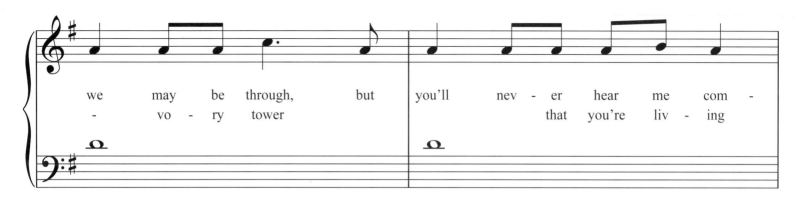

we may be through, but you'll nev - er hear me com -
- vo - ry tower that you're liv - ing

%̸ G

plain." 'Cause I've got friends in low plac - es, where the
in.

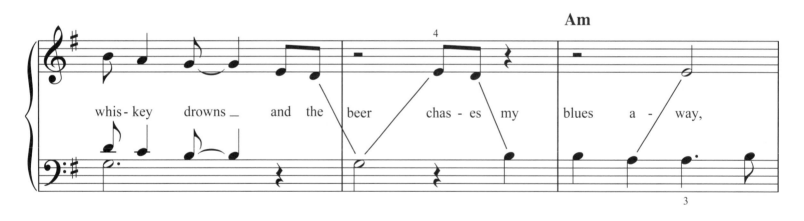

Am

whis - key drowns __ and the beer chas - es my blues a - way,

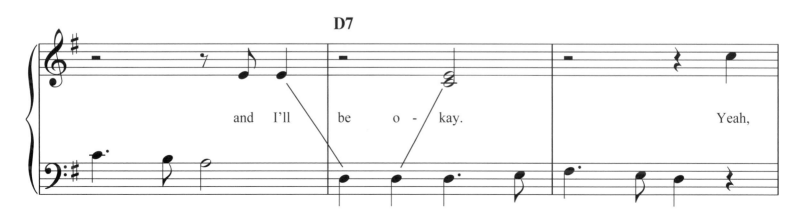

D7

and I'll be o - kay. Yeah,

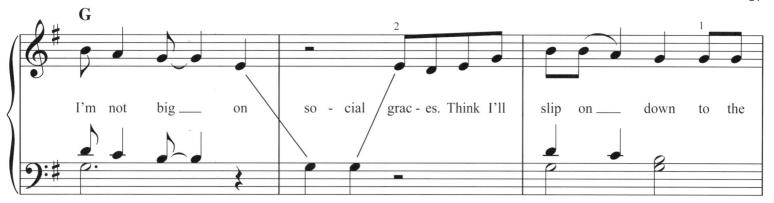

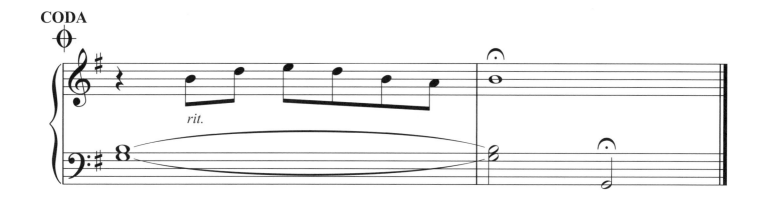

FUNNY HOW TIME SLIPS AWAY

Words and Music by
WILLIE NELSON

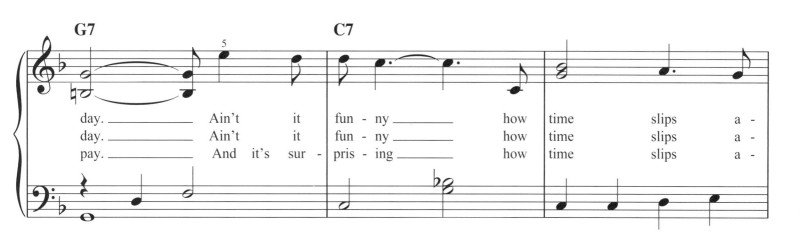

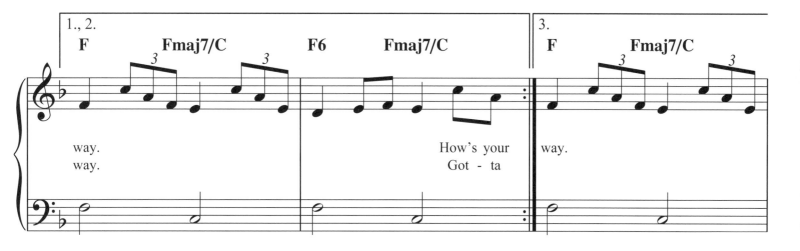

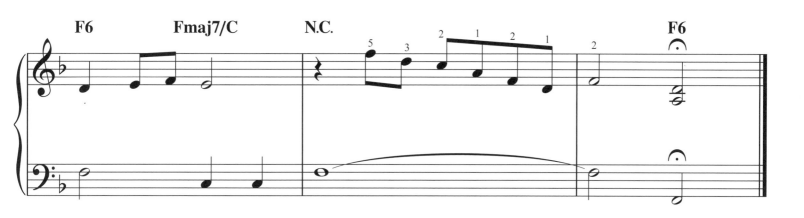

THE GAMBLER

Words and Music by
DON SCHLITZ

warm sum-mer's eve - nin' on a train bound for
son, I've made a life out of read - in' peo - ple's
(See additional lyrics)

no - where, I met up with the gam - bler. We were
fac - es and know-in' what their cards were We by the

both too tired to sleep, so we took turns a
way they held their eyes. And if you don't mind my

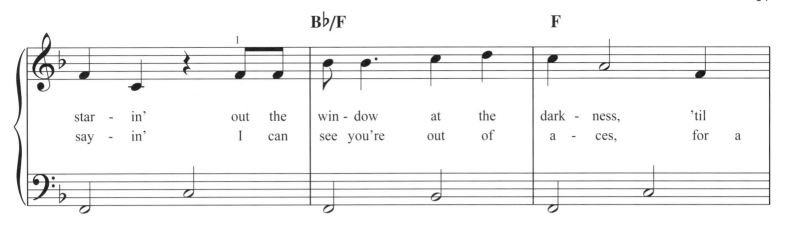

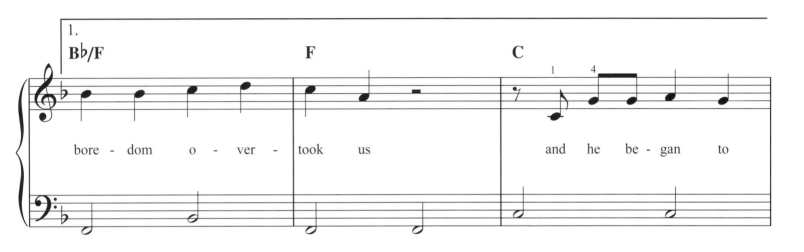

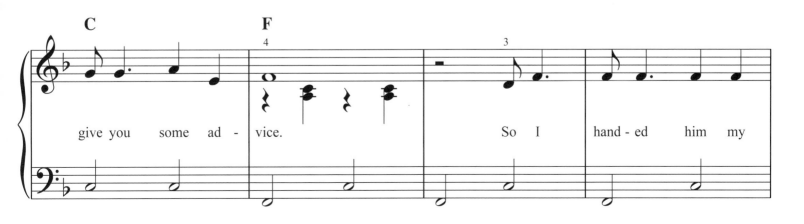

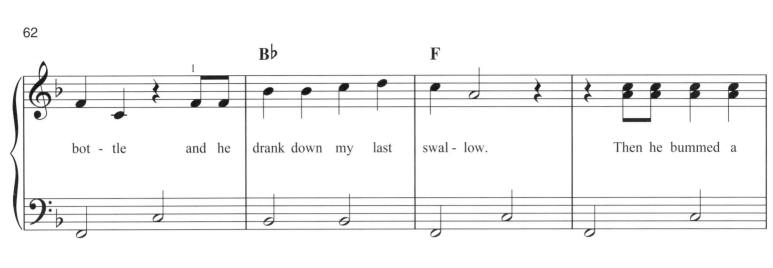

bot - tle   and he | drank down my last | swal - low. | Then he bummed a

cig - a - rette ___   and | asked me for a | light. | And the

night got death - ly | qui - et,   and his | face lost all ex -

pres - sion,   said, "If you're | gon - na play ___ the | game, boy,   you got - ta

Chorus

learn to play ___ it right. You got to know when to hold ___

___ 'em, know when to fold ___ 'em, know when to

walk a - way ___ and know when to run. ___ You nev - er

count your mon - ey when you're sit - tin' at the ta - ble. There'll be

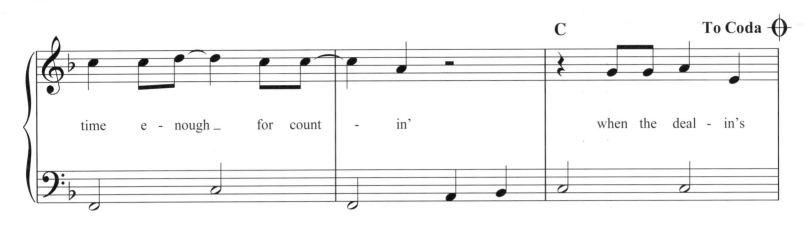

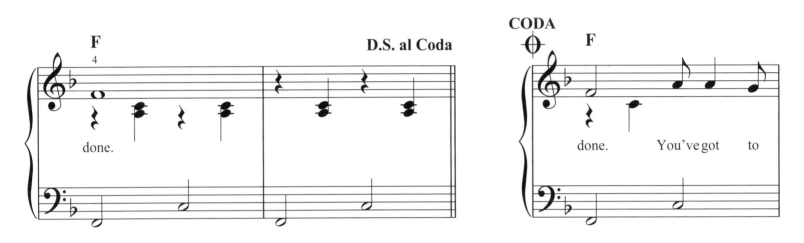

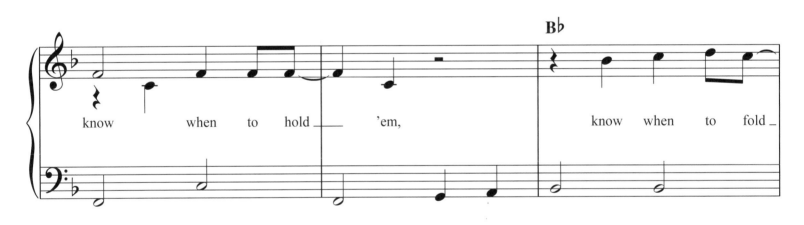

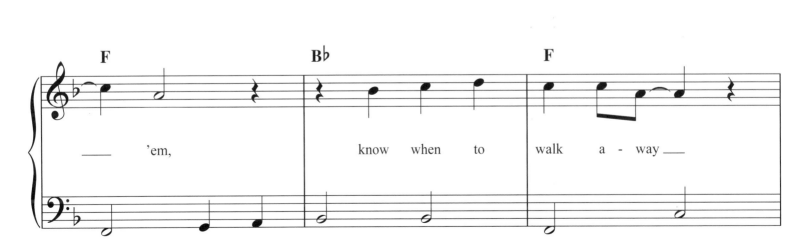

and know when to run. You nev - er count your

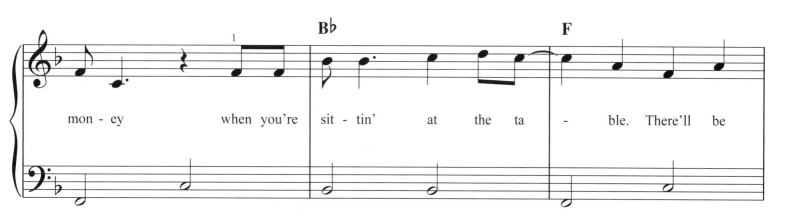

mon - ey when you're sit - tin' at the ta - ble. There'll be

time e - nough _ for count - in' when the deal - in's done.

Additional Lyrics

3. Ev'ry gambler knows that the secret to survivin'
   Is knowin' what to throw away and knowin' what to keep.
   'Cause ev'ry hand's a winner and ev'ry hand's a loser
   And the best that you can hope for is to die in your sleep.
   And when he'd finished speakin', he turned back towards the window
   Crushed out his cigarette and faded off to sleep.
   And somewhere in the darkness, the gambler, he broke even
   But in his final words I found an ace that I could keep.
   Chorus

GRANDPA
(Tell Me 'Bout the Good Old Days)

Words and Music by
JAMIE O'HARA

Medium slow Country

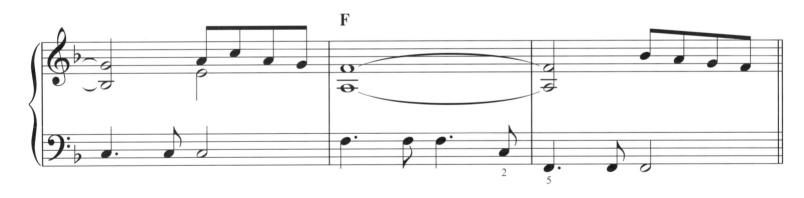

Grand-pa, _____ tell me 'bout the good old days. _____
Grand-pa, _____ ev-'ry-thing is chang-in' fast. _____

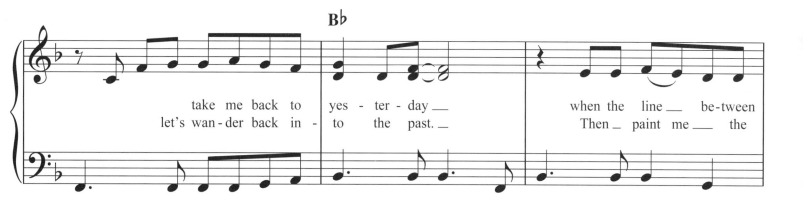

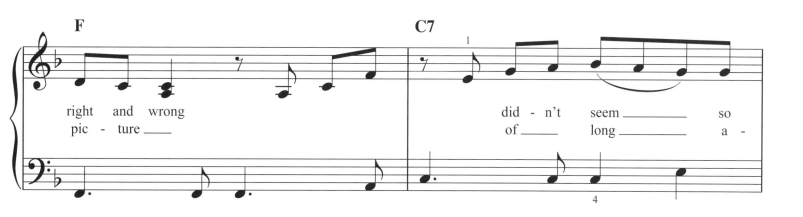

68

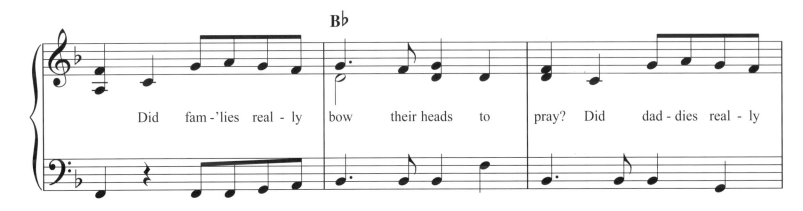

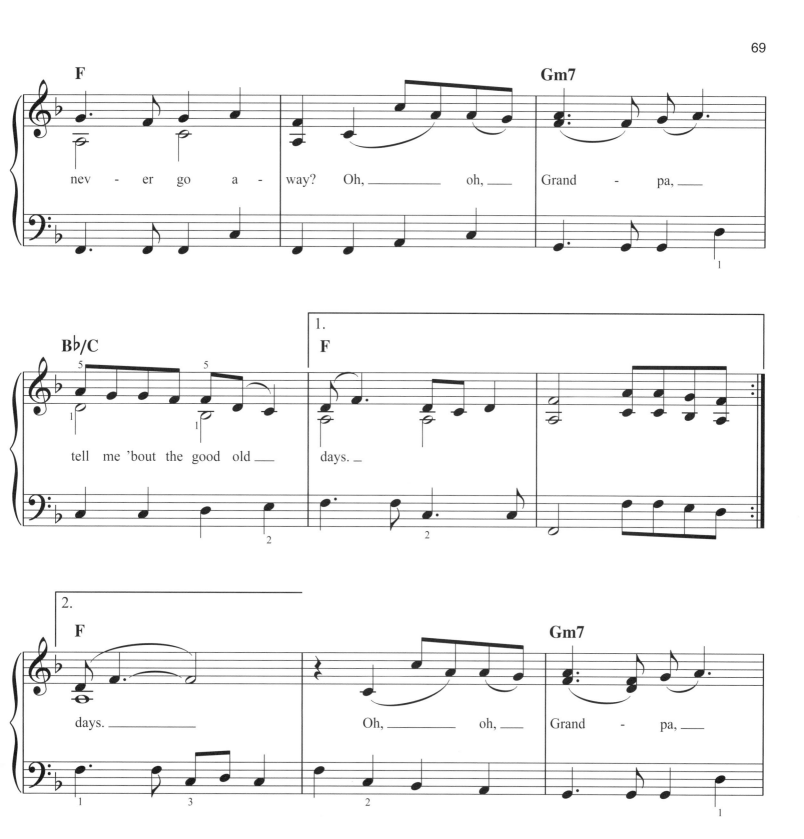

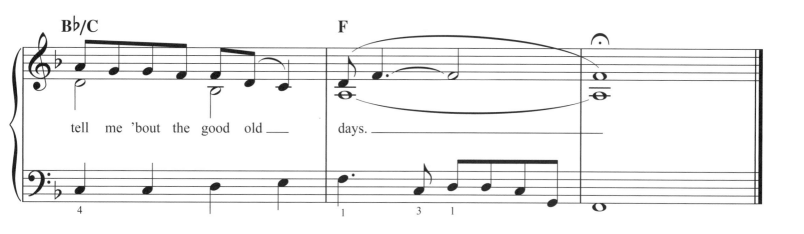

HE STOPPED LOVING HER TODAY

Words and Music by BOBBY BRADDOCK
and CURLY PUTMAN

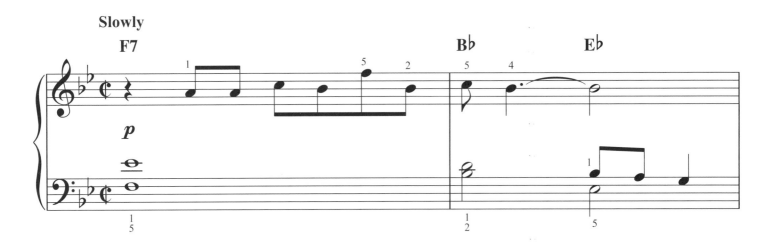

1. He said, "I'll love you 'til I die."
wall,
bed,
4.,5. *(See additional lyrics)*

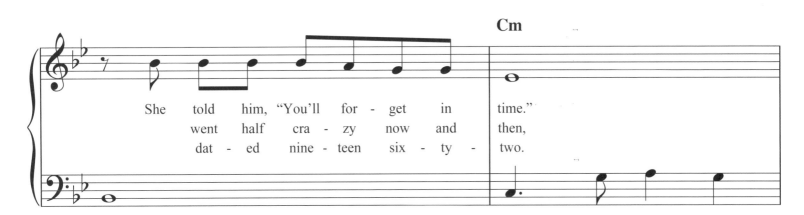

She told him, "You'll for-get in time."
went half cra-zy now and then,
dat-ed nine-teen six-ty-two.

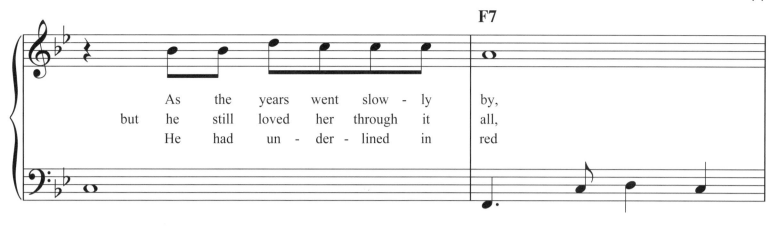

As the years went slow - ly by,
but he still loved her through it all,
He had un - der - lined in red

she still preyed up - on his mind.
hop - ing she'd come back a - gain.
ev - 'ry sin - gle "I love you."

1.-3.

2. He kept her pic - ture on his
3. He kept some let - ters by his
4. I went to see him just to -

4., 5.

Chorus

He stopped lov - ing her to -

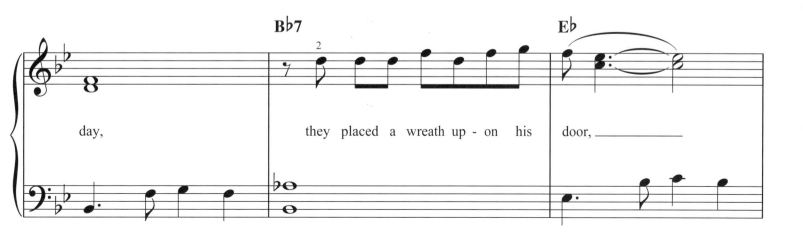

day,

they placed a wreath up - on his door, _____

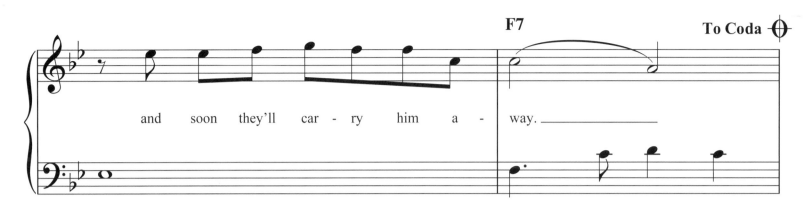

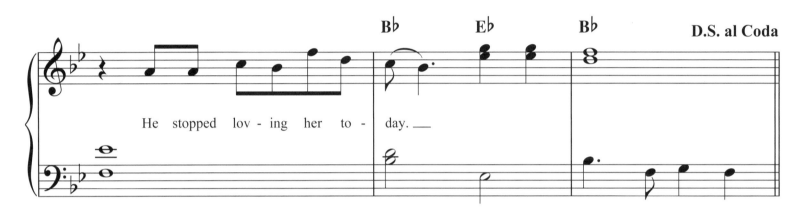

Additional Lyrics

4. I went to see him just today, oh, but I didn't see no tears;
All dressed up to go away, first time I'd seen him smile in years.
Chorus

(Spoken:) 5. *You know, she came to see him one last time; we all wondered if she would.*
And it came running through my mind, this time he's over her for good.
Chorus

GREEN GREEN GRASS OF HOME

Words and Music by
CURLY PUTMAN

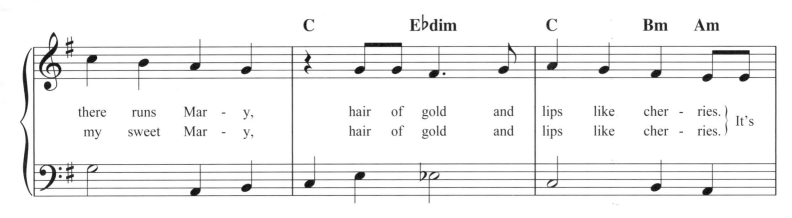

there runs Mar - y,   hair of gold   and   lips like cher - ries.
my sweet Mar - y,   hair of gold   and   lips like cher - ries. It's

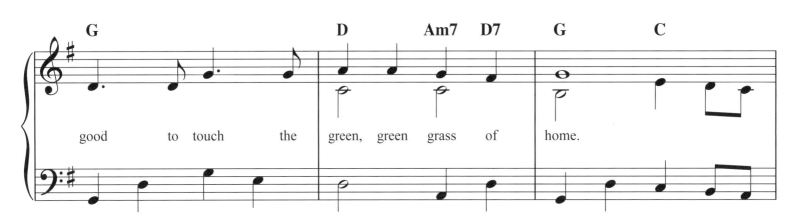

good   to touch   the   green, green grass of   home.

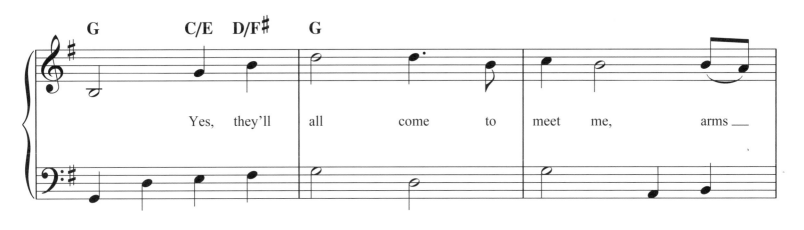

Yes, they'll   all   come   to   meet me,   arms ___

1., 2.

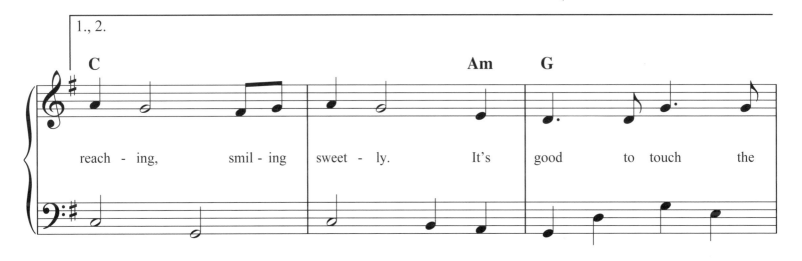

reach - ing,   smil - ing sweet - ly.   It's   good   to touch   the

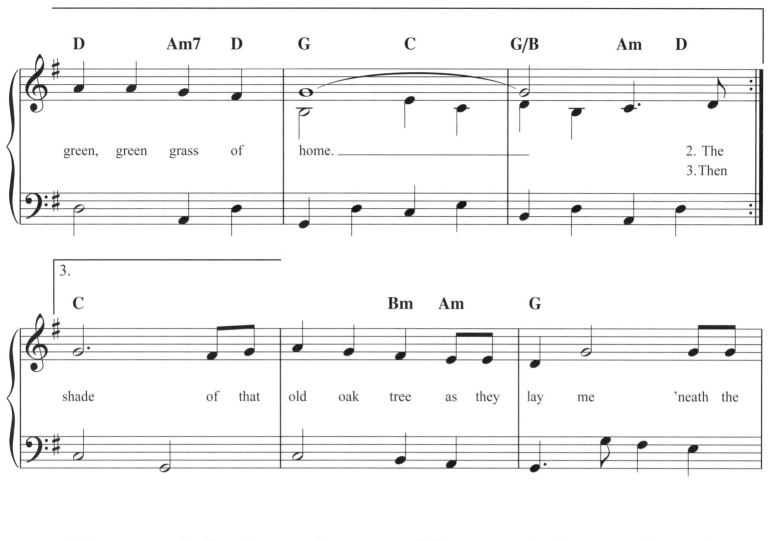

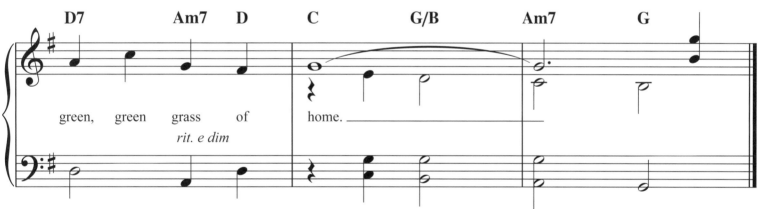

Additional Lyrics

3. Then I awake and look around me
   At four gray walls that surround me,
   And I realize that I was only dreaming.
   For there's a guard and there's a sad old padre,
   Arm in arm we'll walk at daybreak,
   Again I'll touch the green, green grass of home.

   Yes, they'll all come to see me
   In the shade of that old oak tree
   As they lay me 'neath the green, green grass of home.

HAPPY TRAILS
from the Television Series THE ROY ROGERS SHOW

Words and Music by
DALE EVANS

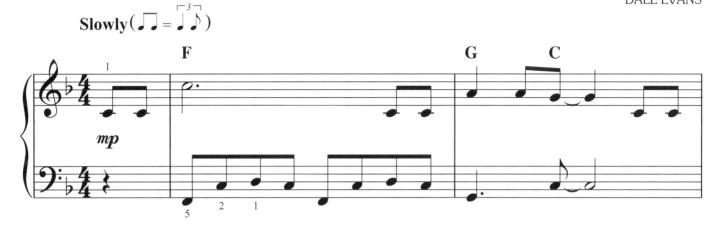

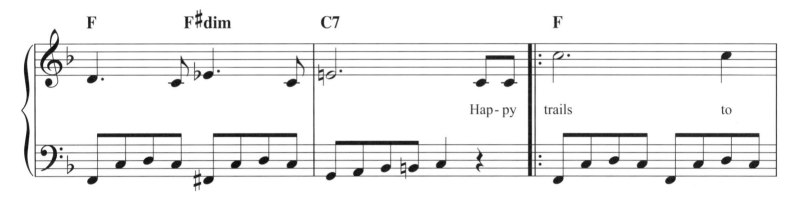

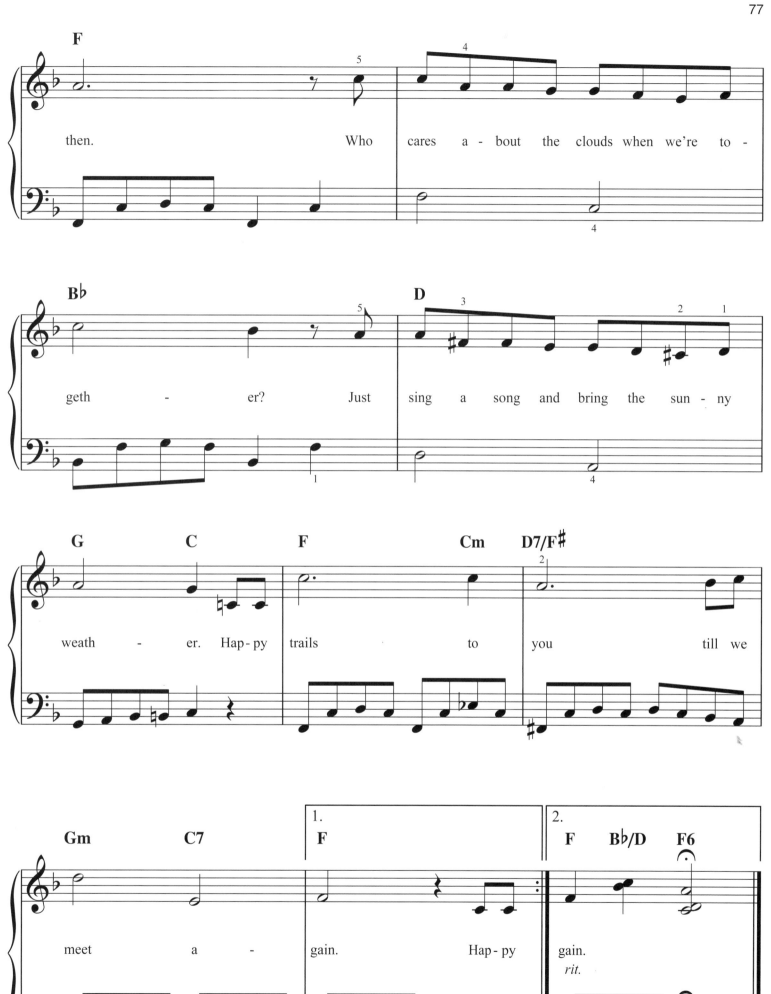

HELP ME MAKE IT THROUGH THE NIGHT

Words and Music by
KRIS KRISTOFFERSON

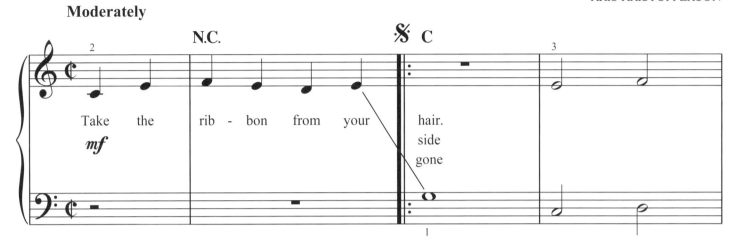

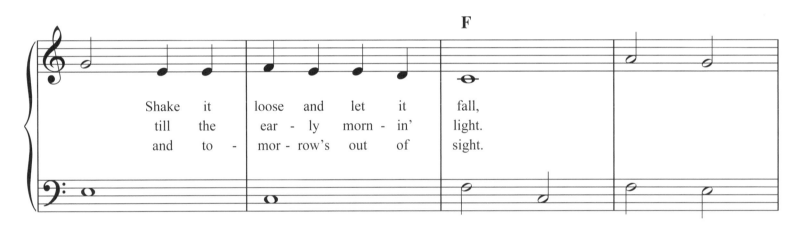

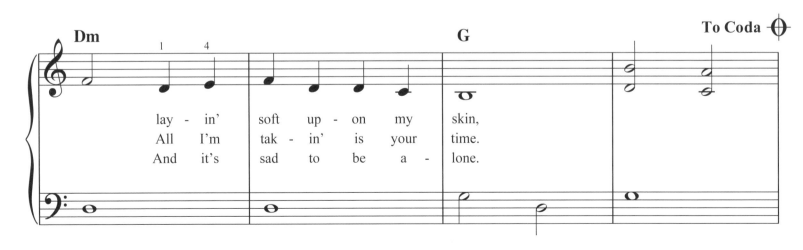

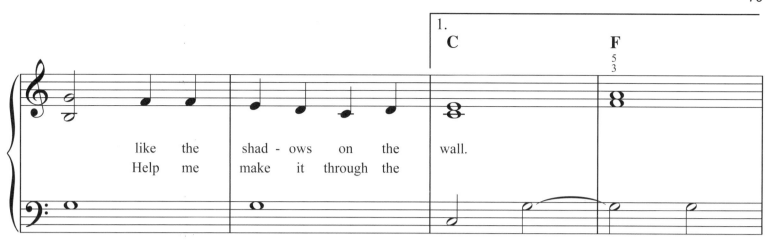

like the shad - ows on the wall.
Help me make it through the

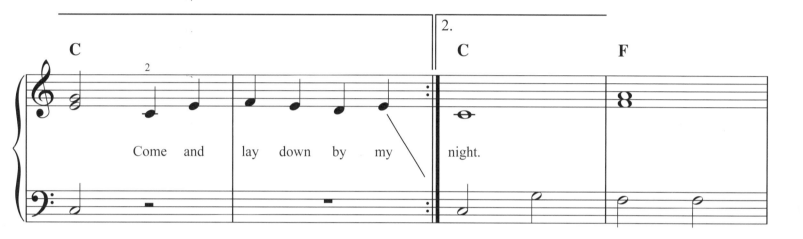

Come and lay down by my night.

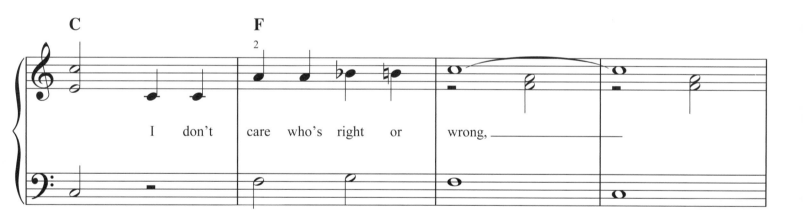

I don't care who's right or wrong, _____

I don't try to un - der - stand. _____

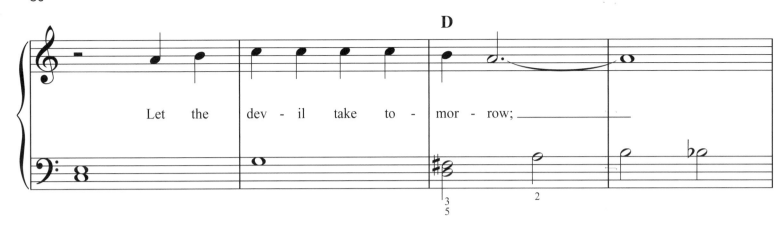

Let the dev - il take to - mor - row; ____

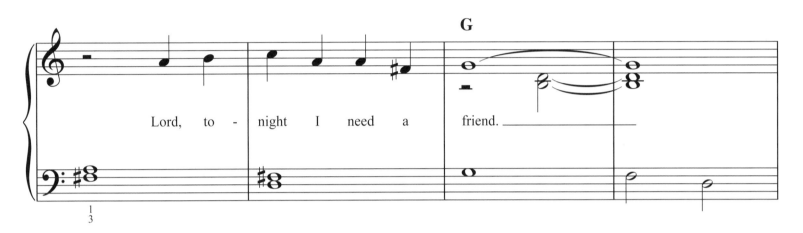

Lord, to - night I need a friend. ____

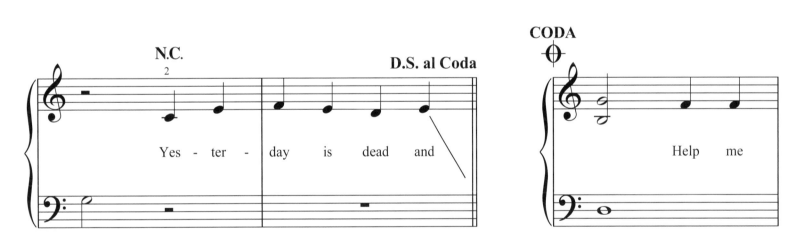

Yes - ter - day is dead and

Help me

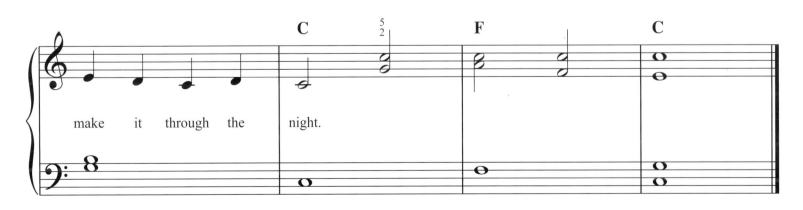

make it through the night.

HEARTACHES BY THE NUMBER

Words and Music by
HARLAN HOWARD

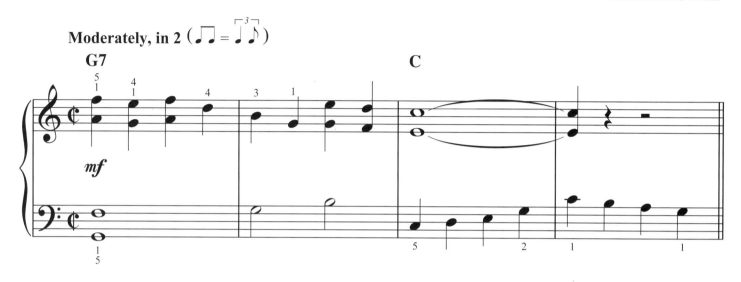

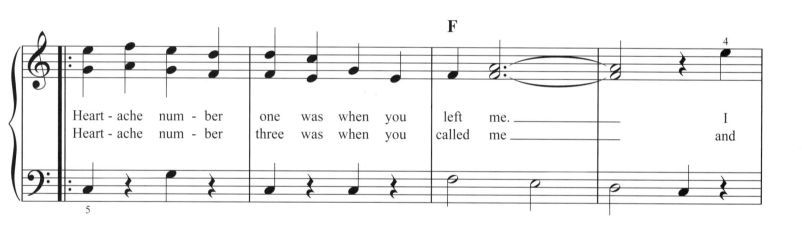

Heart - ache num - ber one was when you left me. _____ I
Heart - ache num - ber three was when you called me _____ and

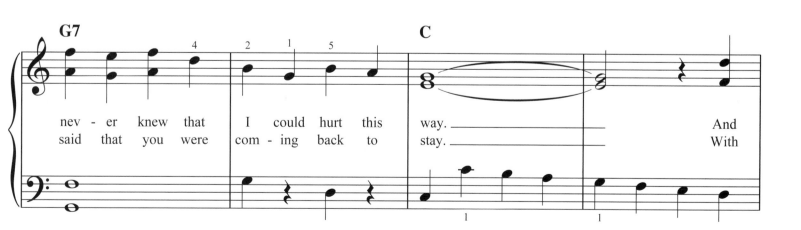

nev - er knew that I could hurt this way. _____ And
said that you were com - ing back to stay. _____ With

heart - ache num - ber / hope - ful heart I two was when you / wait - ed for your came back a - / knock on the gain. door,

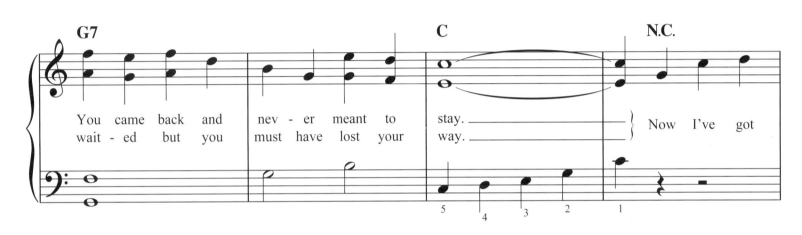

You came back and / wait - ed but you nev - er meant to / must have lost your stay. _____ / way. _____ Now I've got

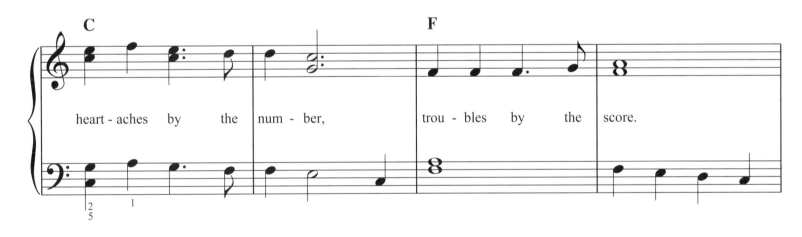

heart - aches by the num - ber, trou - bles by the score.

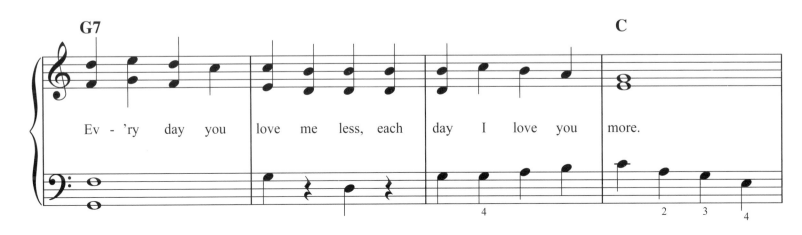

Ev - 'ry day you love me less, each day I love you more.

Yes, I've got heart-aches by the num-ber, a love that I can't

win, but the day that I stop count-ing, that's the day my world will

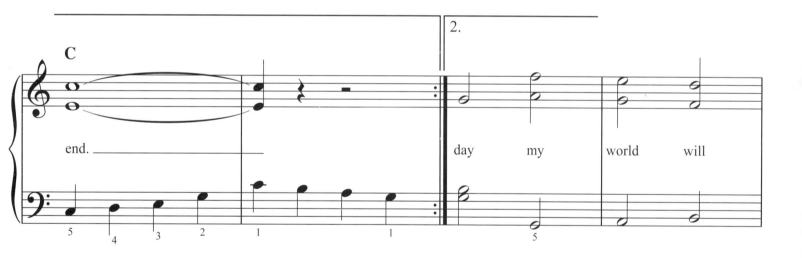

end. day my world will

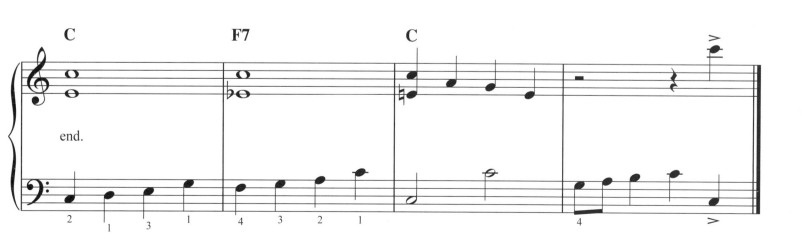

end.

HEY, GOOD LOOKIN'

Words and Music by
HANK WILLIAMS

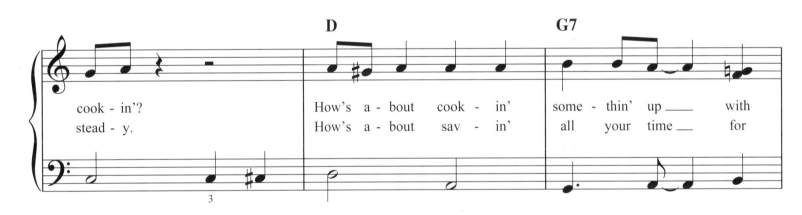

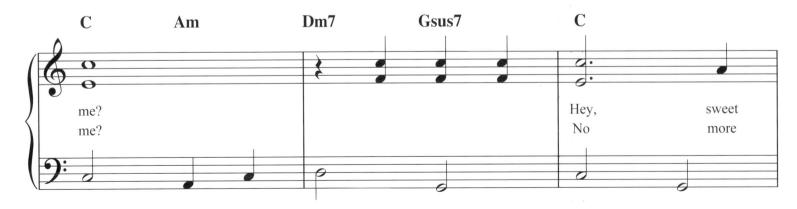

ba - by,
look - in',   I

don't _____ you think
know _____ I've been

may - be,
took - en.

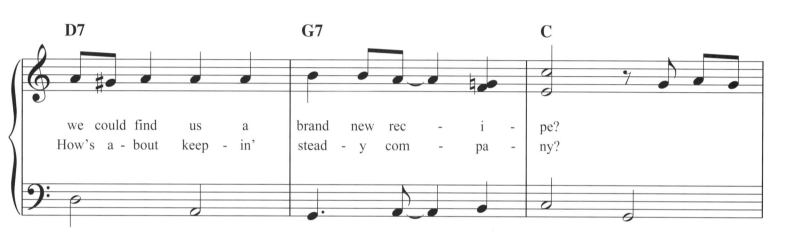

D7   **G7**   **C**

we could find us a
How's a - bout keep - in'

brand new rec - i -
stead - y com - pa -

pe?
ny?

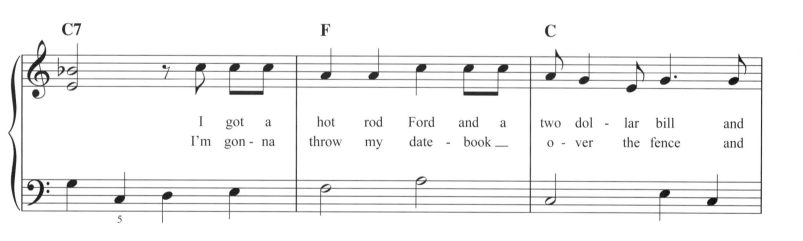

C7   **F**   **C**

I got a
I'm gon - na

hot rod Ford and a
throw my date - book __

two dol - lar bill and
o - ver the fence and

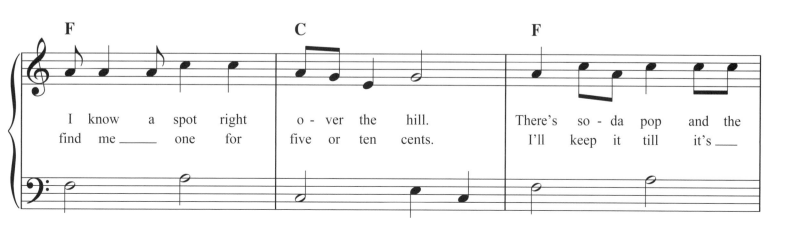

F   **C**   **F**

I know a spot right
find me __ one for

o - ver the hill.
five or ten cents.

There's so - da pop and the
I'll keep it till it's __

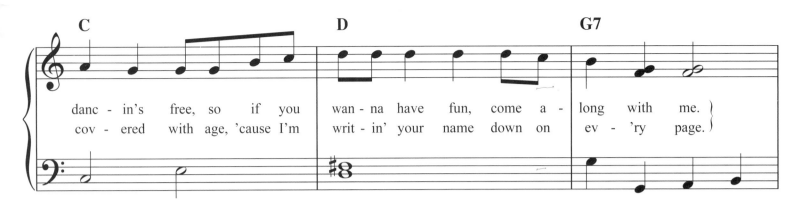

danc - in's free, so if you wan - na have fun, come a - long with me.
cov - ered with age, 'cause I'm writ - in' your name down on ev - 'ry page.

Hey, good look - in', what - cha got

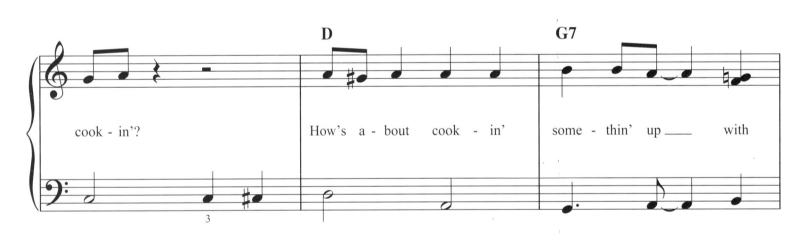

cook - in'? How's a - bout cook - in' some - thin' up ____ with

me? I'm me? *rit.*

I CAN'T HELP IT
(If I'm Still in Love with You)

Words and Music by
HANK WILLIAMS

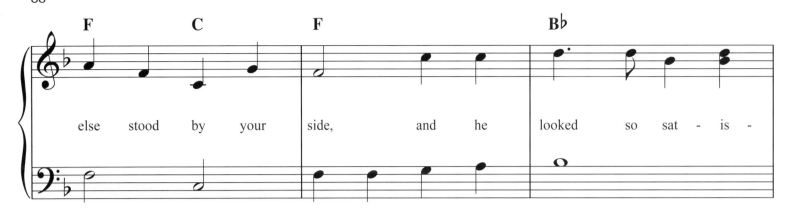

else stood by your   side,   and he   looked so sat - is -

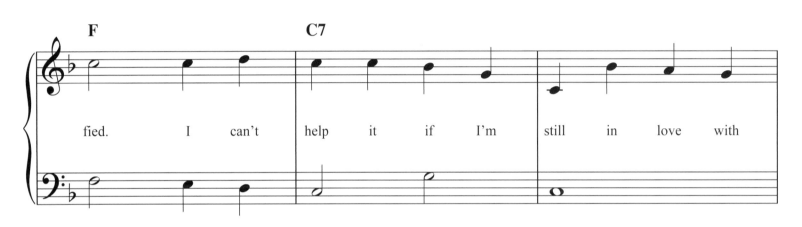

fied.   I   can't   help   it   if   I'm   still   in   love   with

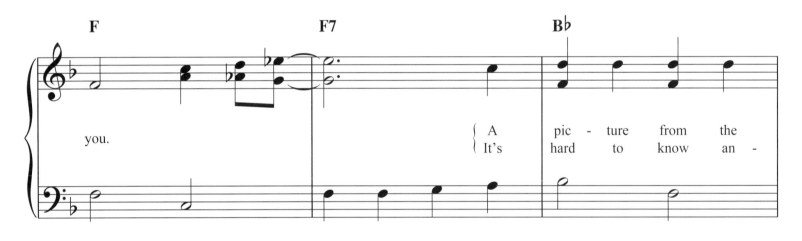

you.

A   pic - ture   from   the
It's   hard   to   know   an -

past came slow - ly   steal - ing _____   as   I
oth - er's lips will   kiss   you _____   and ___

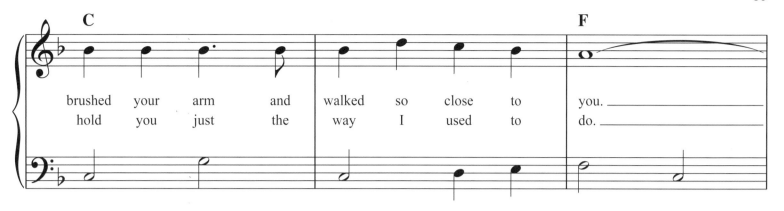

brushed your arm and walked so close to you. ____
hold you just the way I used to do. ____

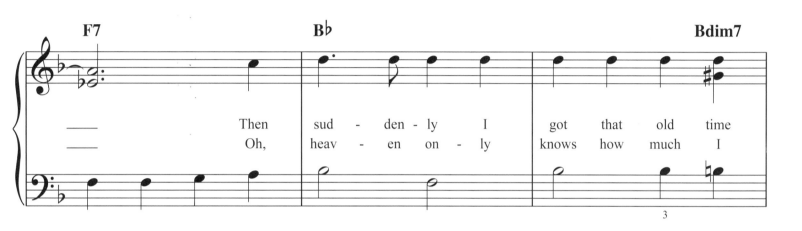

____ Then sud - den - ly I got that old time
____ Oh, heav - en on - ly knows how much I

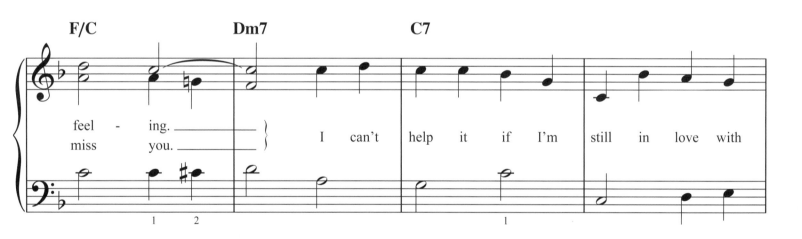

feel - ing. ____ I can't help it if I'm still in love with
miss you. ____

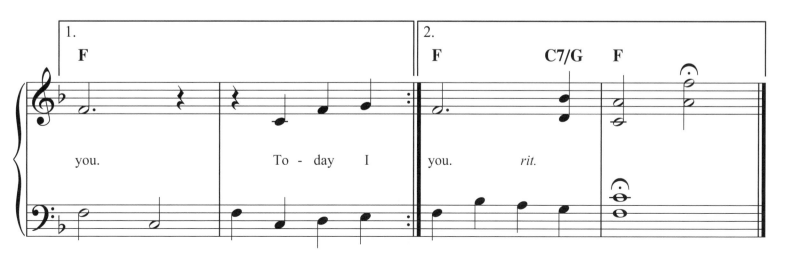

you. To - day I
you. *rit.*

(Hey, Won't You Play)
ANOTHER SOMEBODY DONE SOMEBODY WRONG SONG

Words and Music by LARRY BUTLER
and CHIPS MOMAN

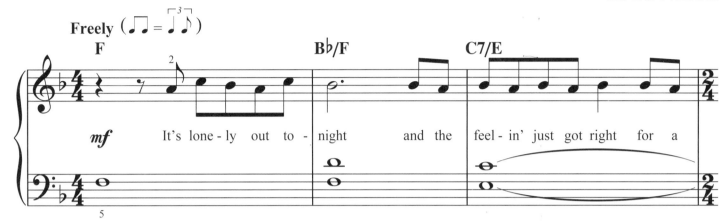

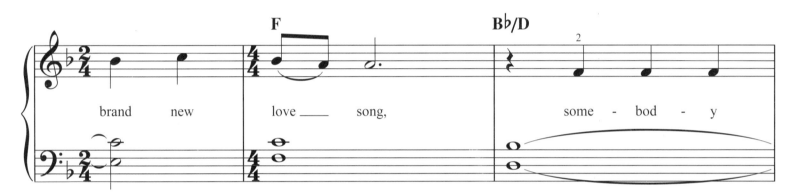

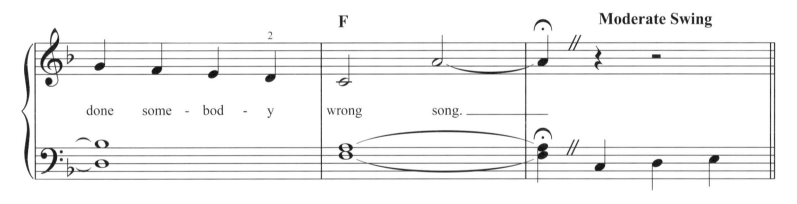

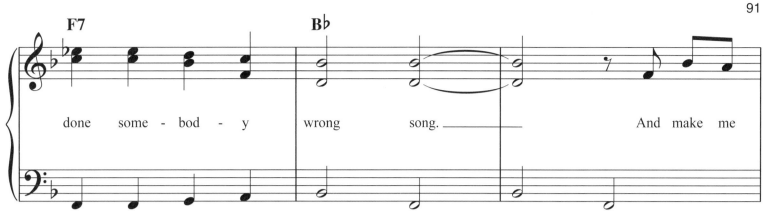

done some-bod-y wrong song._____ And make me

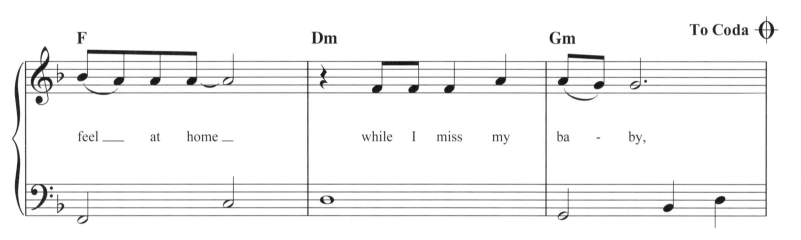

feel ___ at home ___ while I miss my ba - by,

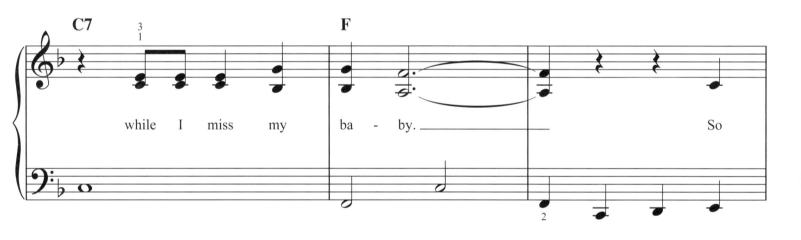

while I miss my ba - by. _____ So

play, play for me a sad mel-o-dy, ___

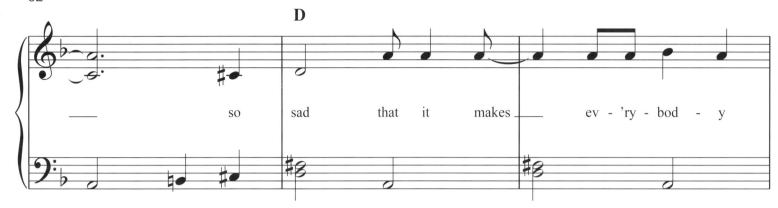

so sad that it makes ___ ev - 'ry - bod - y

cry. ___ A real hurt - in' song ___

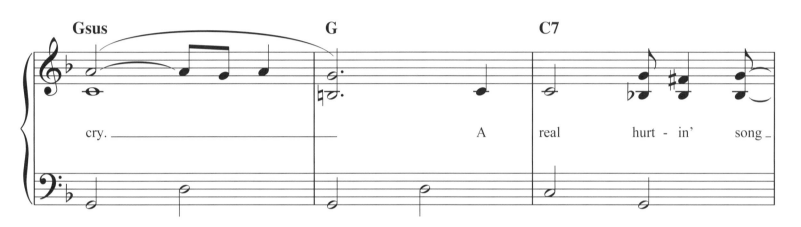

___ a - bout a love that's gone ___ wrong, 'cause

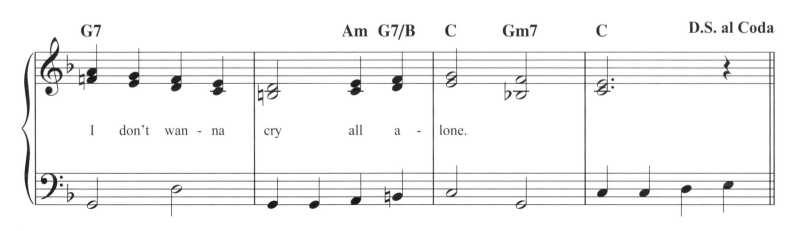

I don't wan - na cry all a - lone.

CODA

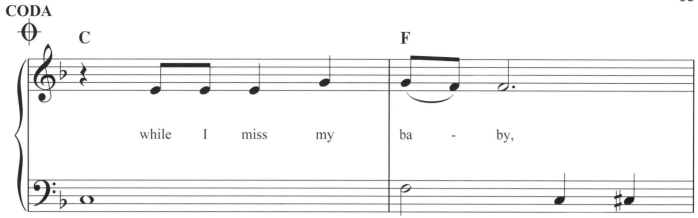

while I miss my ba - by,

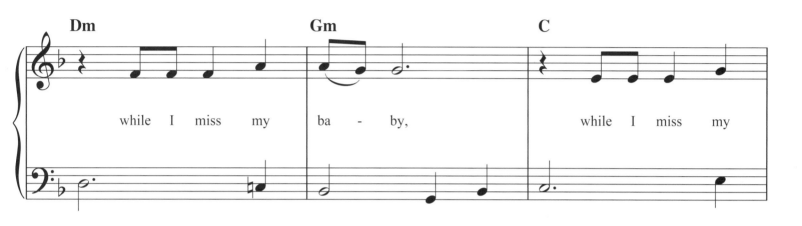

while I miss my ba - by, while I miss my

ba - by, while I miss my ba - by,

while I miss my ba - by.

rit.

I FALL TO PIECES

Words and Music by HANK COCHRAN
and HARLAN HOWARD

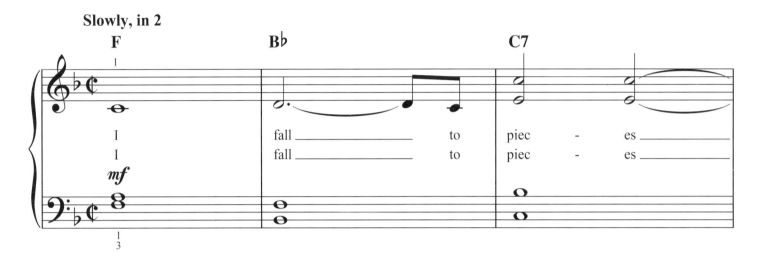

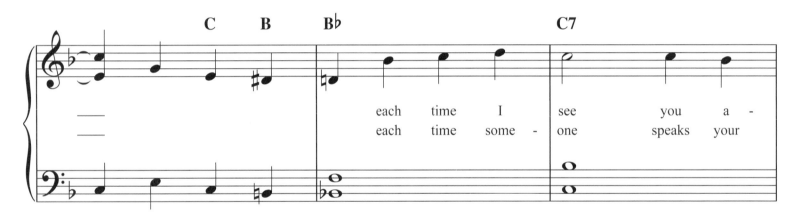

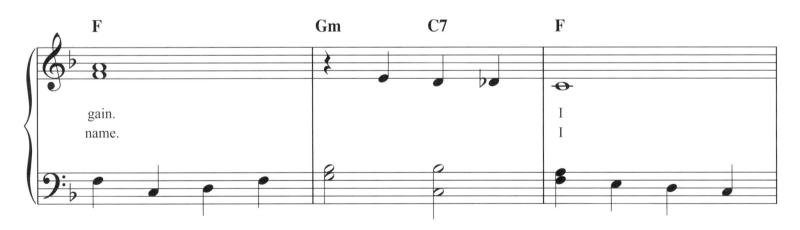

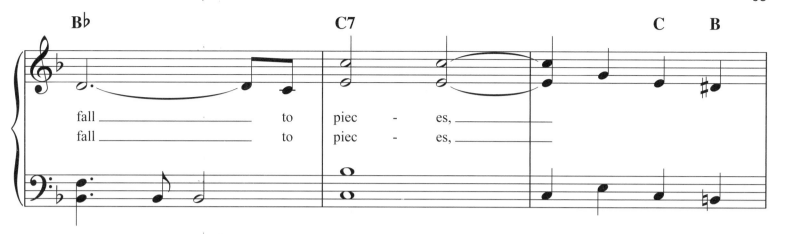

fall _____ to piec - es, _____
fall _____ to piec - es, _____

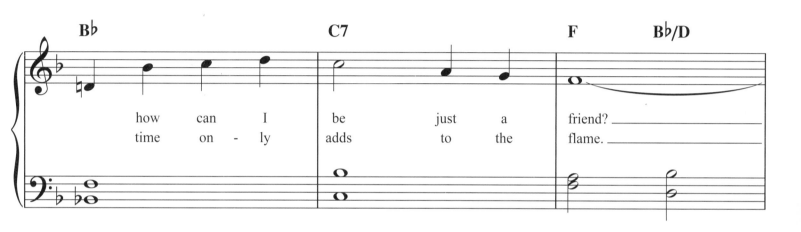

how can I be just a friend? _____
time on - ly adds just to the flame. _____

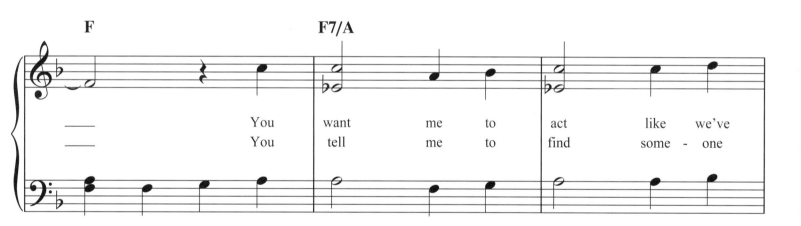

_____ You want me to act like we've
_____ You tell me to find some - one

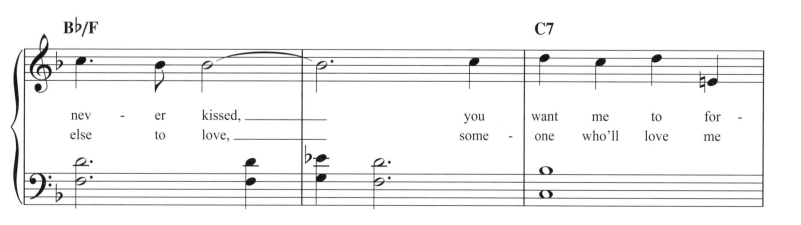

nev - er kissed, _____ you want me to for -
else to love, _____ some - one who'll love me

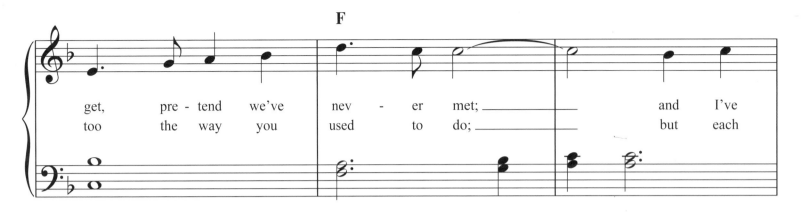

F

get,   pre - tend   we've   nev - er   met; _____   _____   and   I've
too   the   way   you   used   to   do; _____   _____   but   each

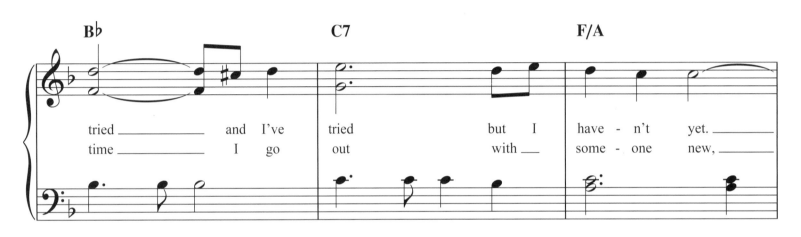

B♭   **C7**   **F/A**

tried _____   and   I've   tried   but   I   have - n't   yet. _____
time _____   I   go   out   with ___   some - one   new,

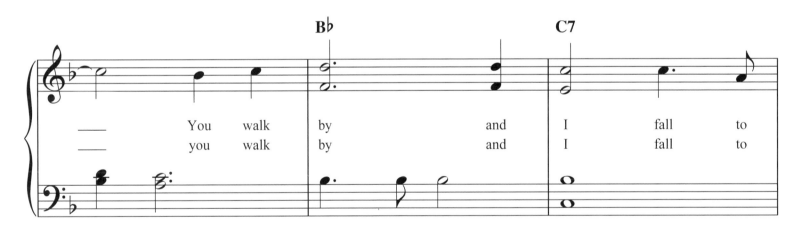

B♭   **C7**

____   You   walk   by   and   I   fall   to
____   you   walk   by   and   I   fall   to

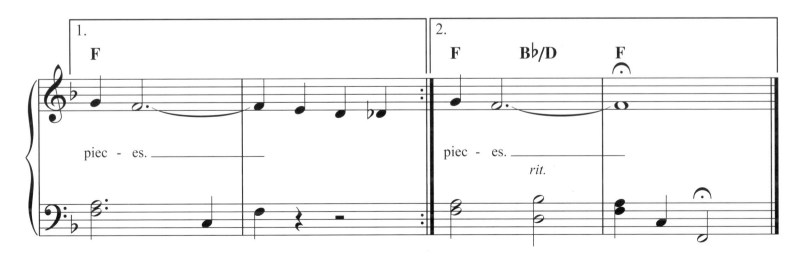

1.   **F** | **2.**   **F**   **B♭/D**   **F**

piec - es. _____ | piec - es. _____
                                              rit.

JAMBALAYA
(On the Bayou)

Words and Music by
HANK WILLIAMS

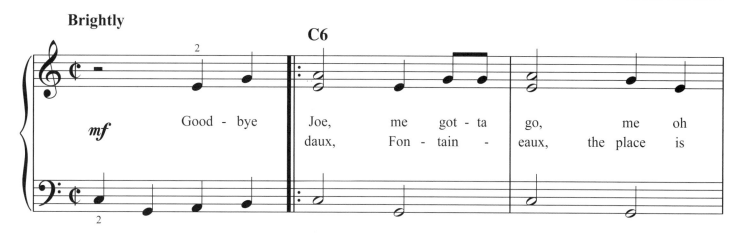

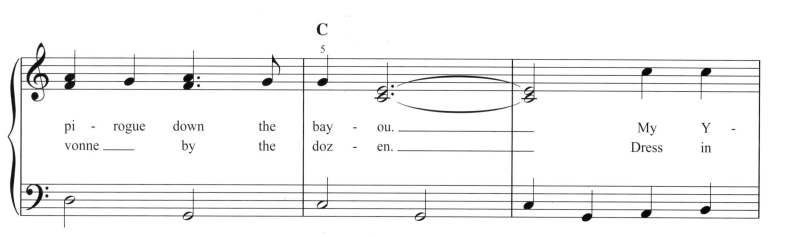

vonne, the sweet - est one, me oh my oh. _____
style and go hog wild, me oh my oh. _____

_____ Son of a gun, we'll have big fun on the
_____ Son of a gun, we'll have big fun on the

bay - ou. }
bay - ou. }   Jam - ba - la - ya and a craw - fish

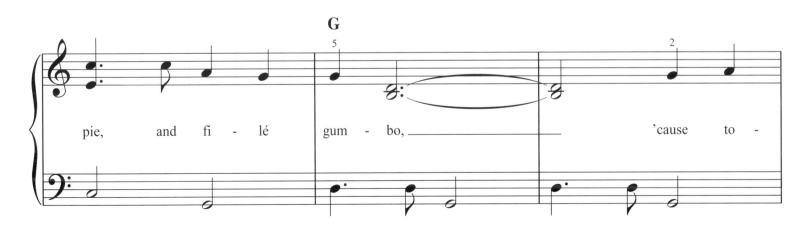

pie, and fi - lé gum - bo, _____ 'cause to -

night I'm gon - na see my ma cher a - mi - o. ___

___ Pick gui - tar, fill fruit jar and be

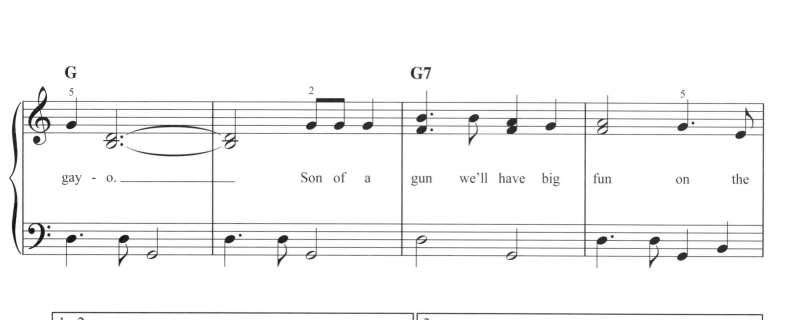

gay - o. ___ Son of a gun we'll have big fun on the

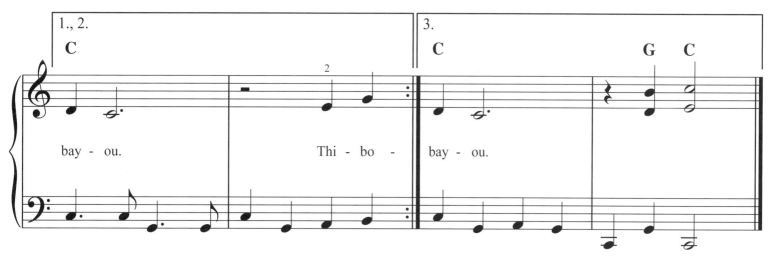

1., 2.	3.

bay - ou.   Thi - bo - bay - ou.

I WALK THE LINE

Words and Music by
JOHN R. CASH

Bright Country 2-beat

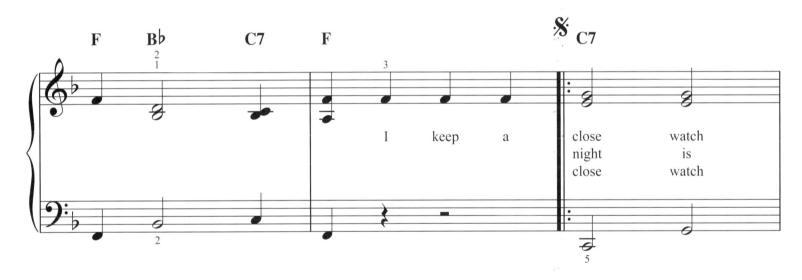

I keep a
close watch
night is
close watch

on this heart of mine.
dark and day is light,
on this heart of mine.
I keep my
I keep you
I keep my

C7

eyes wide o - pen all the time.
on my mind both all day and night.
eyes wide o - pen all the time.

F

F7

I keep the ends out for the tie that
And hap - pi - ness I've known proves that that it's
I keep the ends out for proves the tie that

B♭

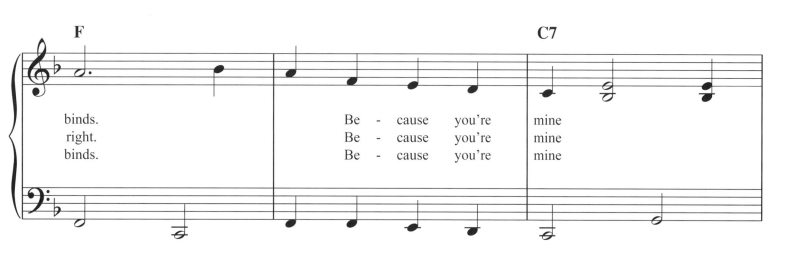

F

binds.
right.
binds.

C7

Be - cause you're mine
Be - cause you're mine
Be - cause you're mine

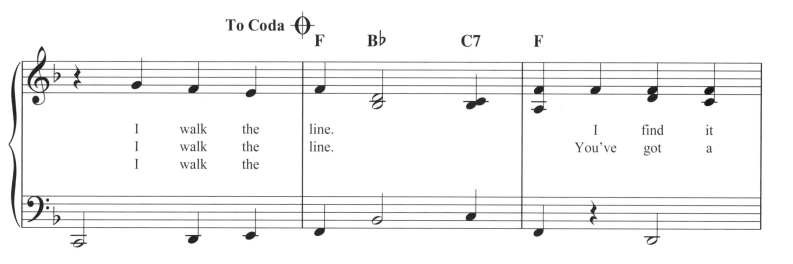

To Coda ⊕ **F**   **B♭**   **C7**   **F**

I walk the line.
I walk the line.
I walk the

I find it
You've got a

ver - y
way to

eas - y to be
keep me on your

true.
side.

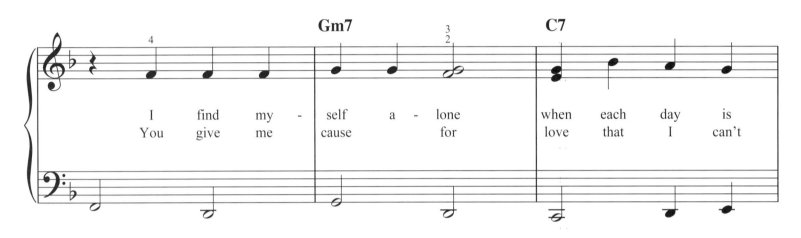

I find my - self a - lone
You give me cause a - lone for

when each day is
love that I can't

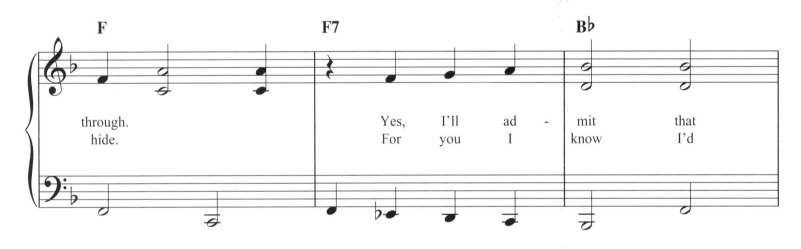

through.
hide.

Yes, I'll ad - mit that
For you I know that I'd

I'm a fool for
e - ven turn the

you.
tide.

Be - cause you're
Be - cause you're

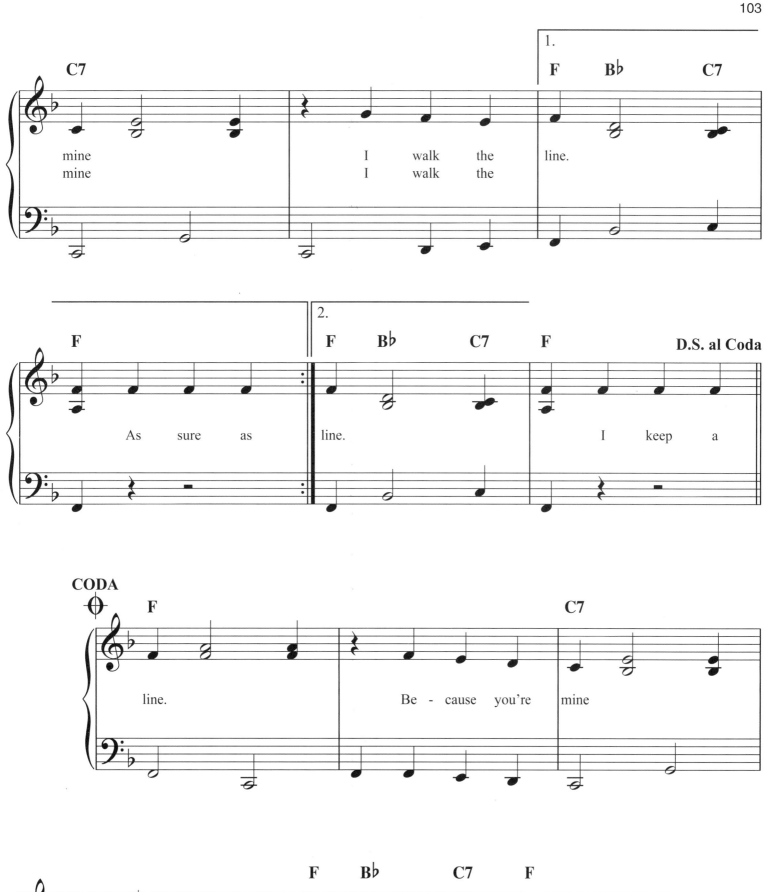

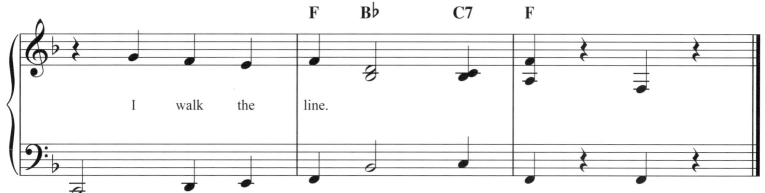

I WILL ALWAYS LOVE YOU

Words and Music by
DOLLY PARTON

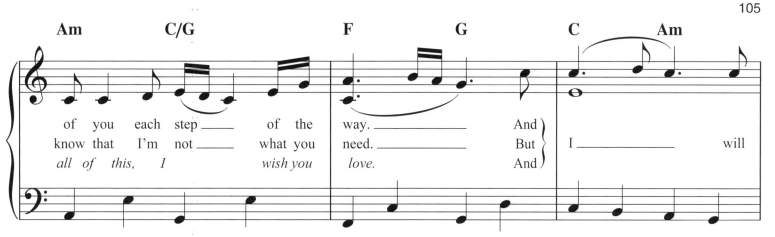

of you each step ____ of the way. ____ And
know that I'm not ____ what you need. ____ But
all of this, I *wish you* *love.* And

al - ways ____ love ____ you. ____ I ____ will al - ways ____ love ____

1., 2.

you.

3.

Bit - ter -
(Spoken:) I

you. ____

I will al - ways love you.

IT'S ONLY MAKE BELIEVE

Words and Music by CONWAY TWITTY
and JACK NANCE

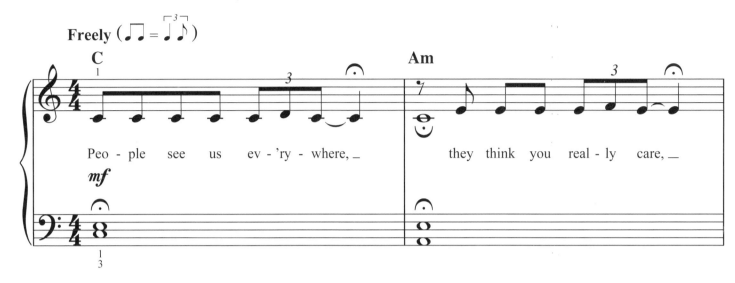

Peo - ple see us ev - 'ry - where, __ they think you real - ly care, __

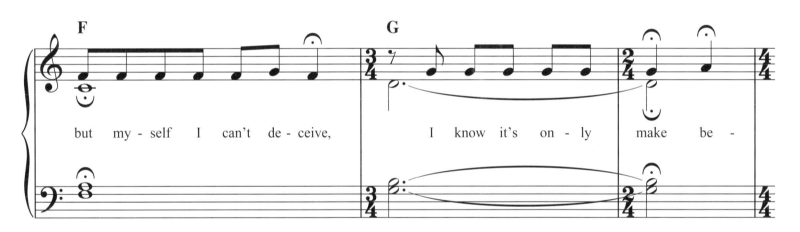

but my - self I can't de - ceive, I know it's on - ly make be -

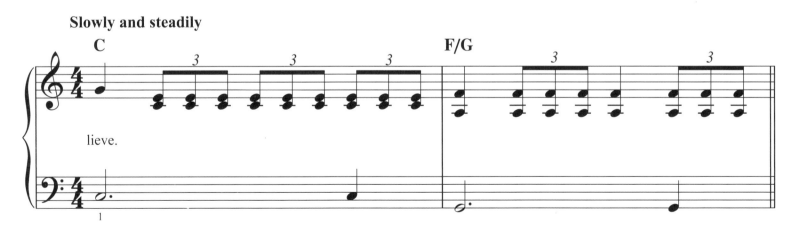

lieve.

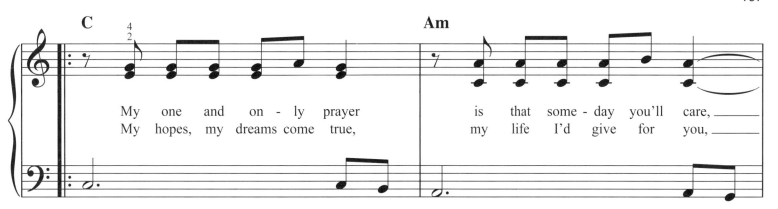

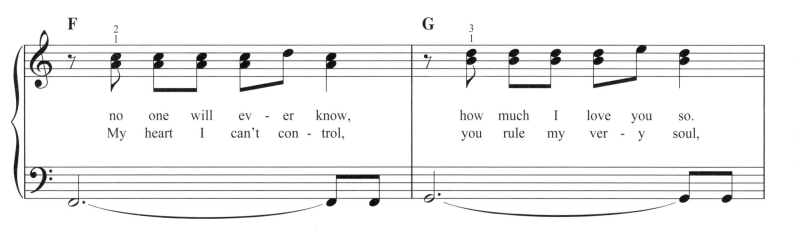

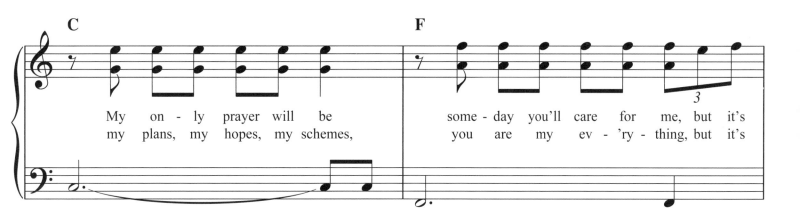

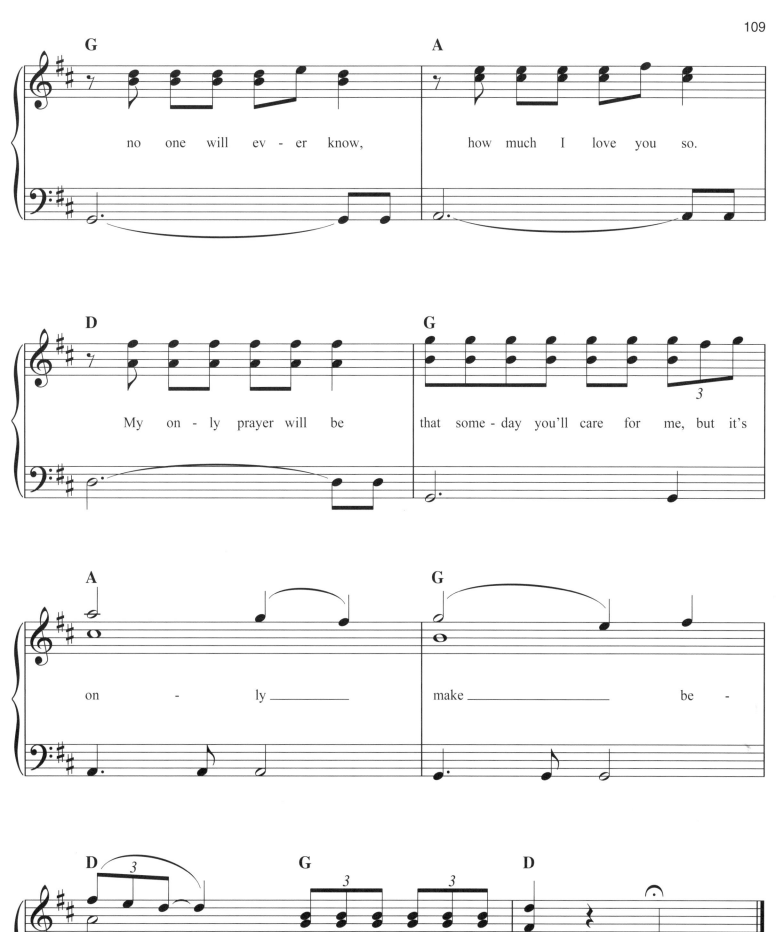

no one will ev - er know, how much I love you so.

My on - ly prayer will be that some - day you'll care for me, but it's

on - ly make be -

lieve.

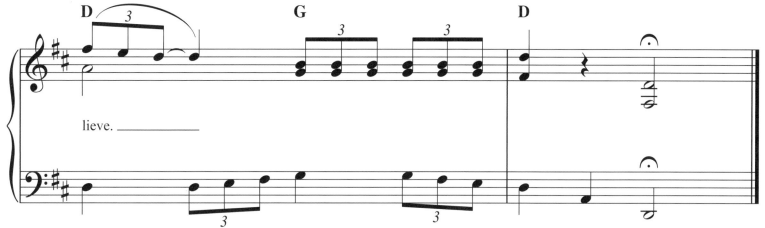

KING OF THE ROAD

Words and Music by
ROGER MILLER

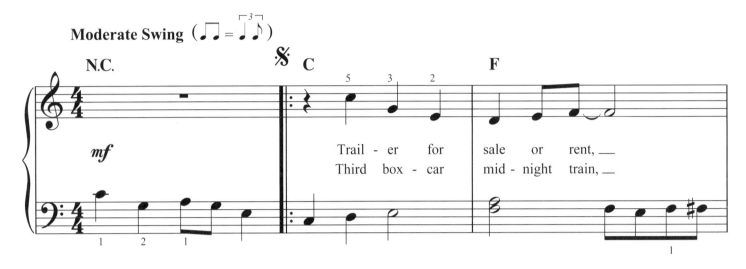

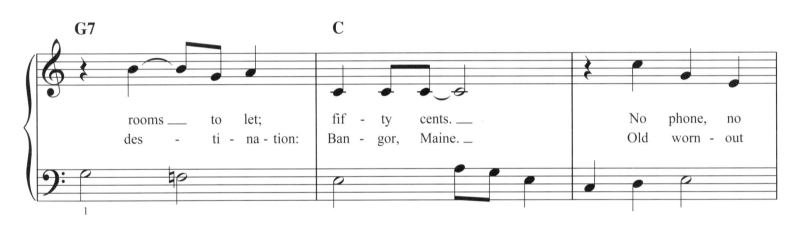

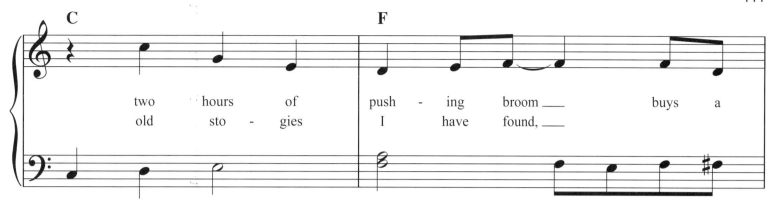

two hours of / old sto - gies   push - ing broom ___ buys a / I have found, ___

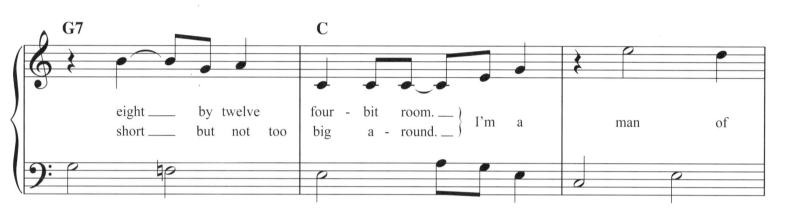

eight ___ by twelve / short ___ but not too   four - bit room. ___ / big a - round. ___   I'm a   man of

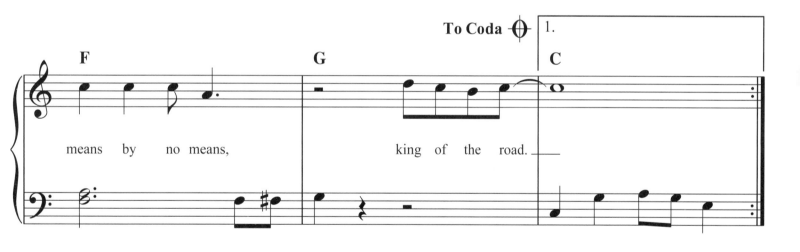

To Coda 1.

means by no means,   king of the road. ___

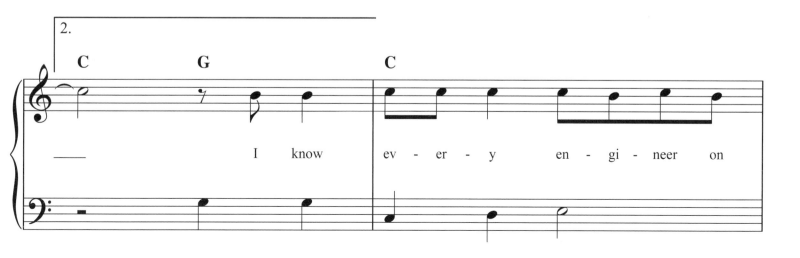

2.

___   I know   ev - er - y en - gi - neer on

ev - er - y train, ____ all of the chil - dren and

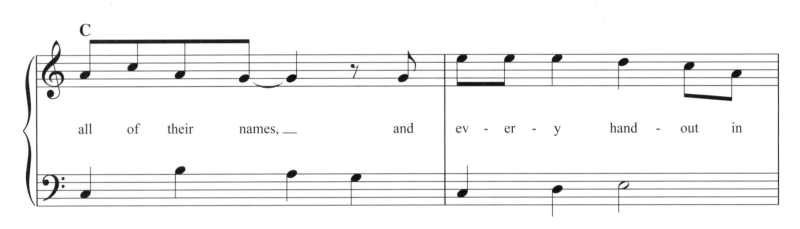

all of their names, ___ and ev - er - y hand - out in

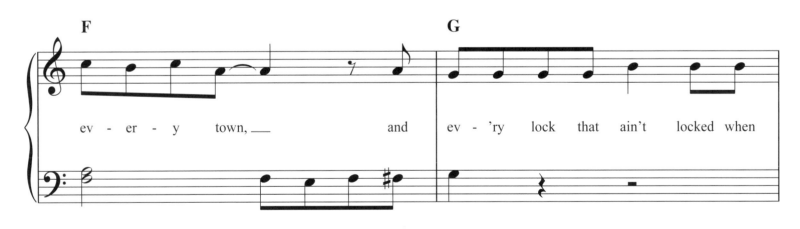

ev - er - y town, ___ and ev - 'ry lock that ain't locked when

D.S. al Coda
(Verse 1)

CODA

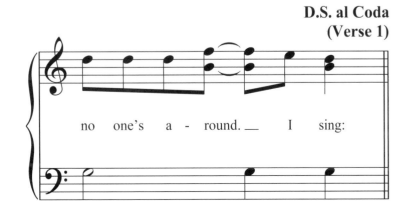

no one's a - round. ___ I sing:

MAMMAS DON'T LET YOUR BABIES GROW UP TO BE COWBOYS

Words and Music by ED BRUCE
and PATSY BRUCE

let 'em pick gui - tars and drive them old

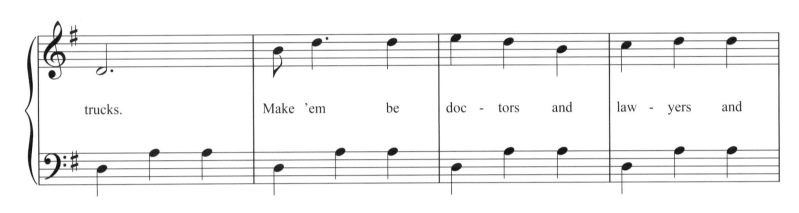

trucks. Make 'em be doc - tors and law - yers and

such. Mam - mas, _____ don't let your

ba - bies grow up ___ to be cow - boys,

'cause they'll nev - er stay ___ home, and they're

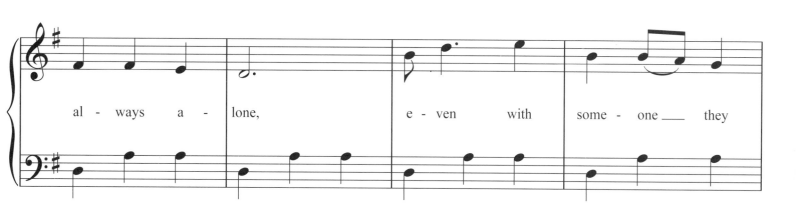

al - ways a - lone, e - ven with some - one ___ they

love.

{ A
{ A

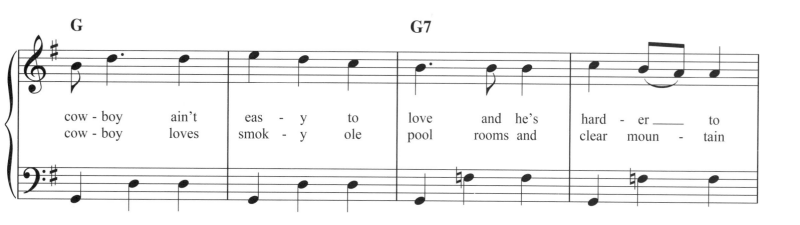

cow - boy ain't eas - y to love and he's hard - er ___ to
cow - boy loves smok - y ole pool rooms and clear moun - tain

C

hold.
morn - ings,

And it means

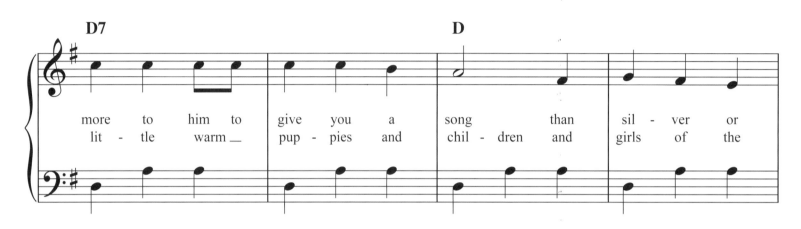

D7　　　　　　　　　　　　　　　　　**D**

more to him to　give you a　song than　sil - ver or
lit - tle warm __　pup - pies and　chil - dren and　girls of the

G　　　　　　　　　　　　　　　　　**D**

gold.
night.

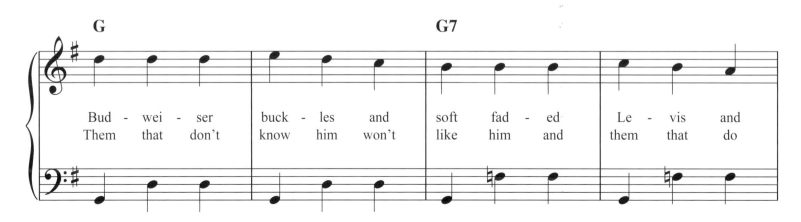

G　　　　　　　　　　　　　　**G7**

Bud - wei - ser　buck - les and　soft fad - ed　Le - vis and
Them that don't　know him won't　like him and　them that do

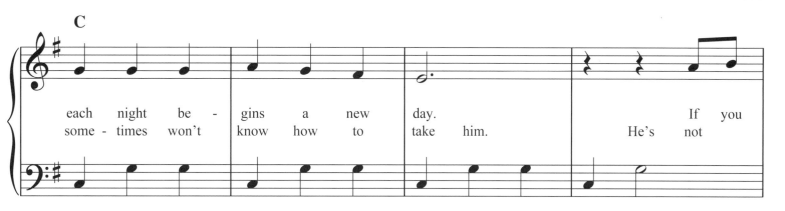

each night be - gins a new day. If you
some - times won't know how to take him. He's not

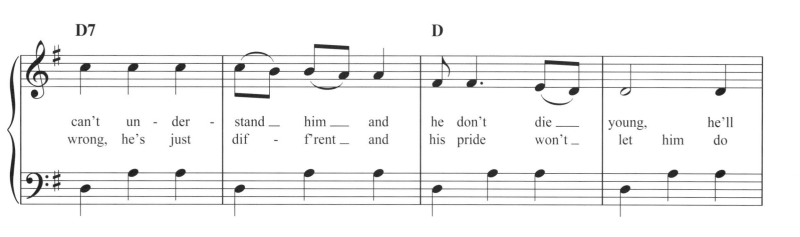

can't un - der - stand __ him __ and he don't die __ young, he'll
wrong, he's just dif - f'rent __ and his pride won't __ let him do

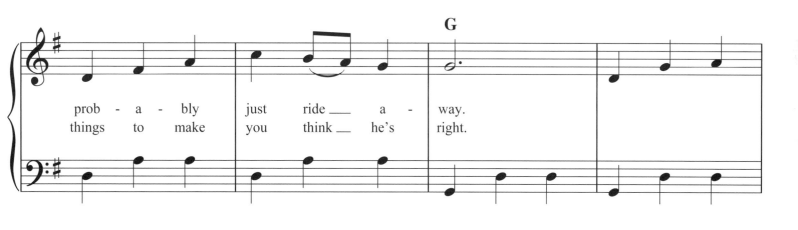

prob - a - bly just ride __ a - way.
things to make you think __ he's right.

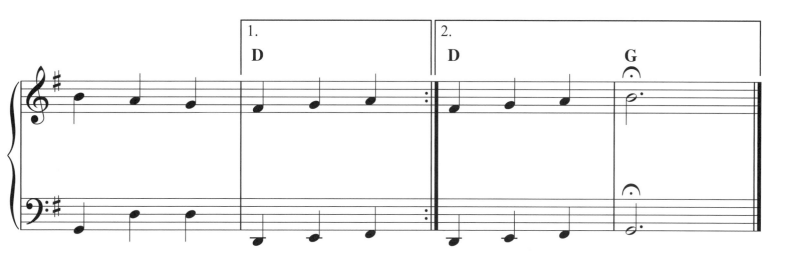

MAKE THE WORLD GO AWAY

Words and Music by
HANK COCHRAN

F   **G7**

Make the world go a - way, and get it off ___ my ___

C   **F**

shoul - ders. Say the things you used to say,

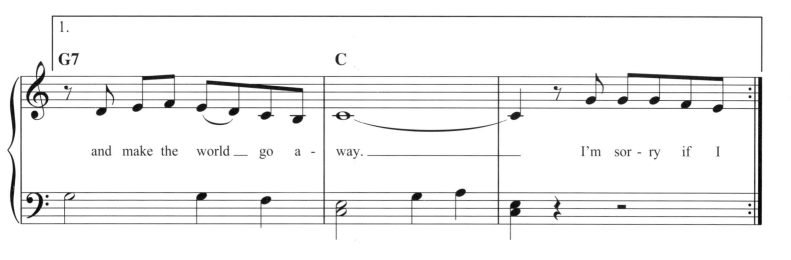

1.

G7   **C**

and make the world __ go a - way. _____ I'm sor - ry if I

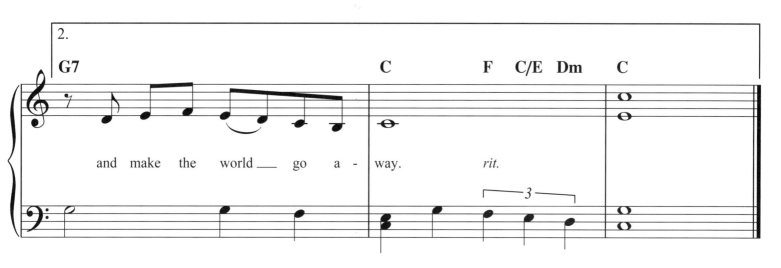

2.

G7   **C**   **F C/E Dm**   **C**

and make the world __ go a - way. *rit.*

____ 3 ____

ON THE ROAD AGAIN

Words and Music by
WILLIE NELSON

Moderately, in 2

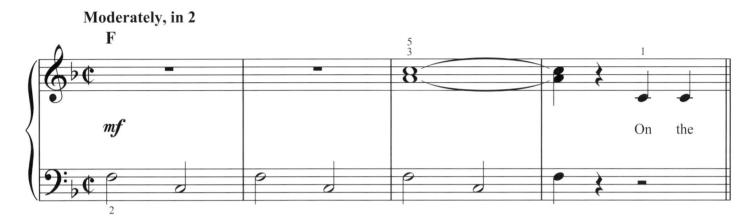

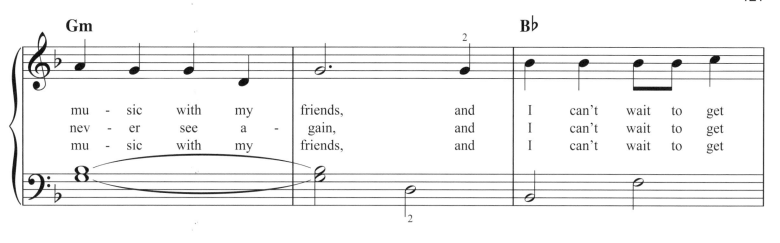

mu - sic with my friends, and I can't wait to get
nev - er see a - gain, and I can't wait to get
mu - sic with my friends, and I can't wait to get

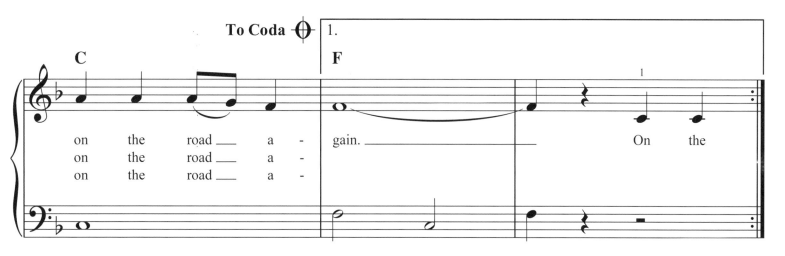

To Coda

on the road ___ a - gain. ___ On the
on the road ___ a -
on the road ___ a -

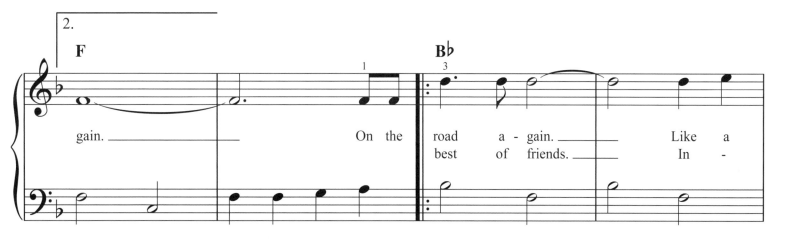

gain. ___ On the road a - gain. ___ Like a
best of friends. ___ In -

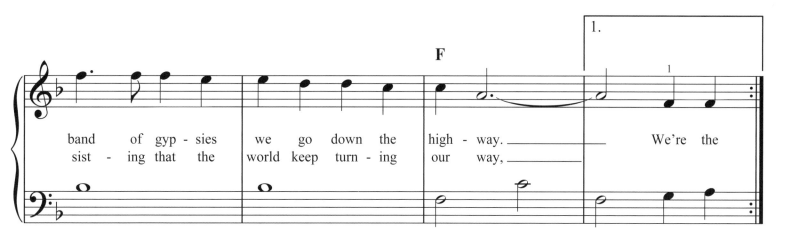

band of gyp - sies we go down the high - way. ___ We're the
sist - ing that the world keep turn - ing our way,

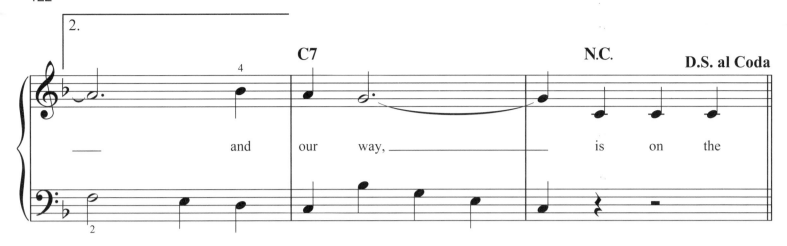

and our way, _____ is on the

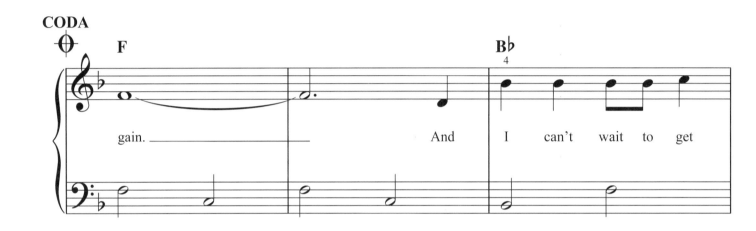

gain. _____ And I can't wait to get

on the road __ a - gain. _____

MOUNTAIN MUSIC

Words and Music by
RANDY OWEN

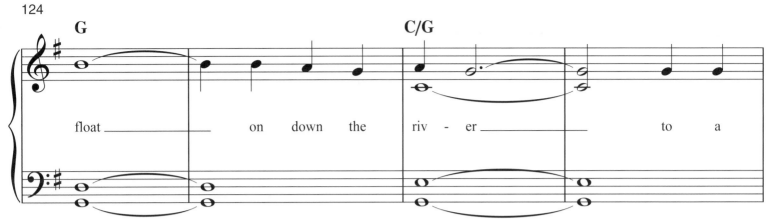

float _____ on down the riv - er _____ to a

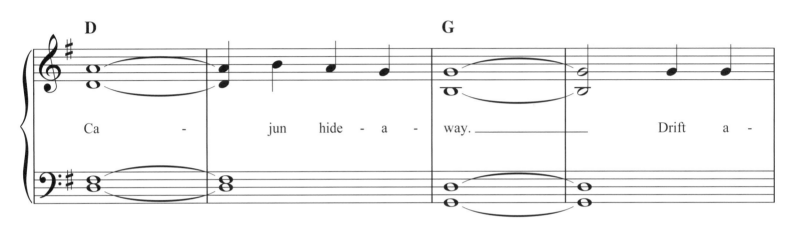

Ca - jun hide - a - way. _____ Drift a -

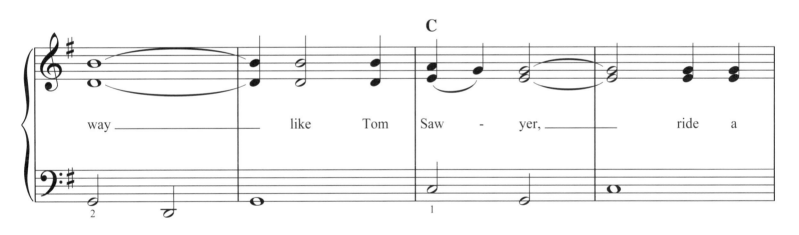

way _____ like Tom Saw - yer, _____ ride a

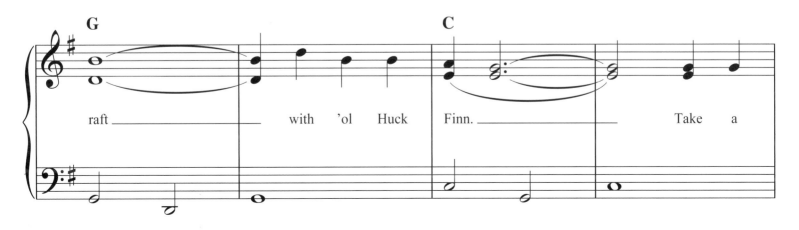

raft _____ with 'ol Huck Finn. _____ Take a

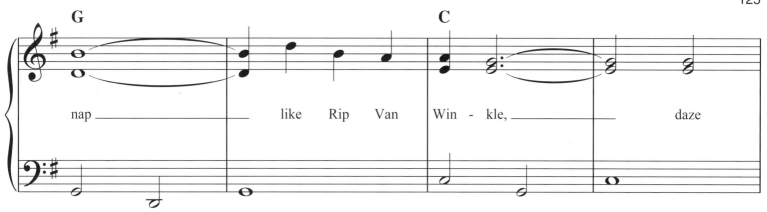

nap _____ like Rip Van Win - kle, _____ daze

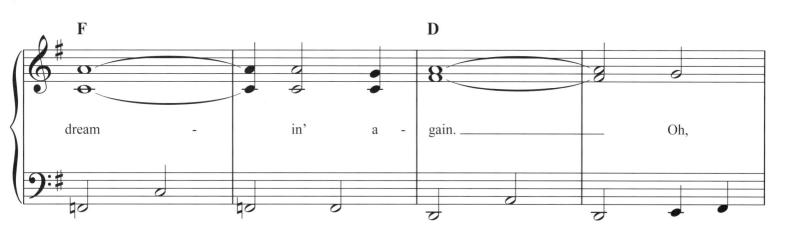

dream - in' a - gain. _____ Oh,

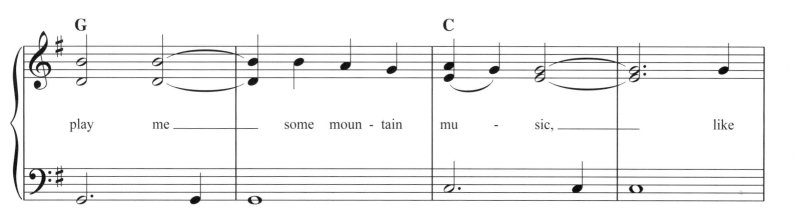

play me _____ some moun - tain mu - sic, _____ like

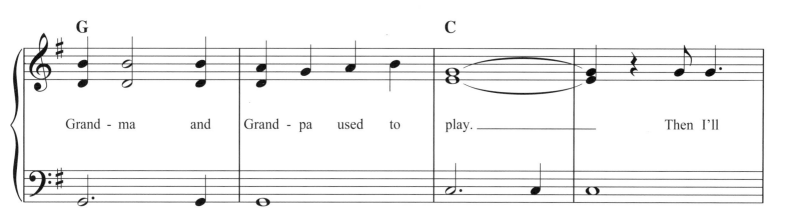

Grand - ma and Grand - pa used to play. _____ Then I'll

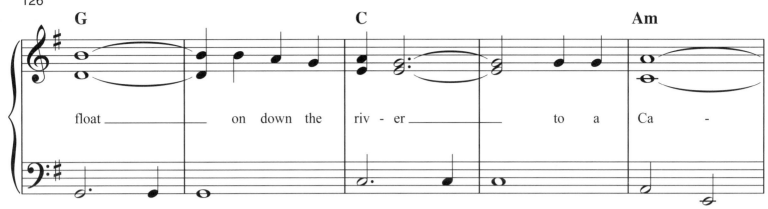

float _____ on down the riv - er _____ to a Ca -

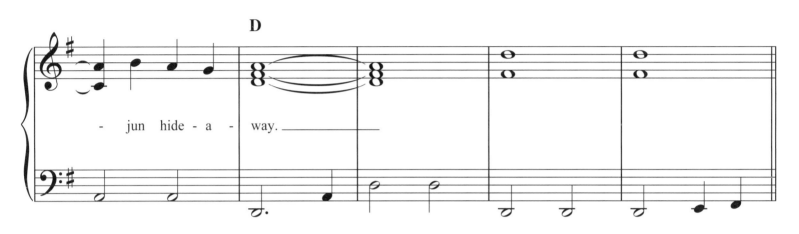

- jun hide - a - way. _____

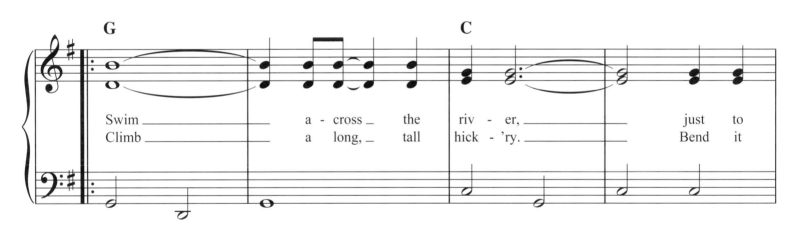

Swim _____ a - cross __ the riv - er, _____ just to
Climb _____ a long, __ tall hick - 'ry. _____ Bend it

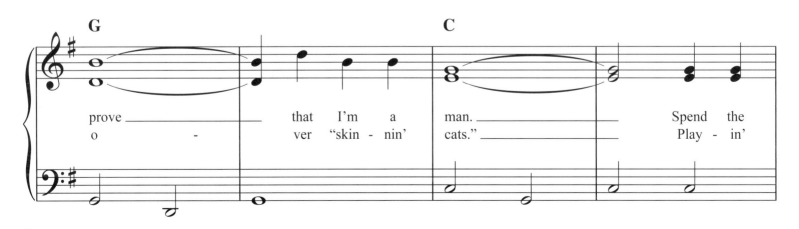

prove _____ that I'm a man. _____ Spend the
o - _____ ver "skin - nin' cats." _____ Play - in'

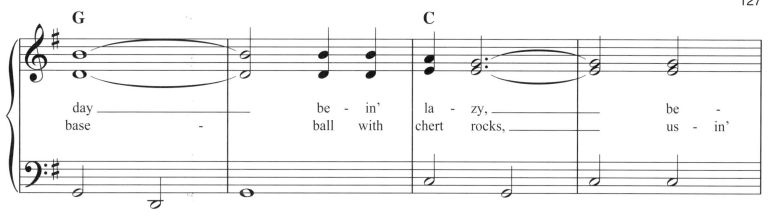

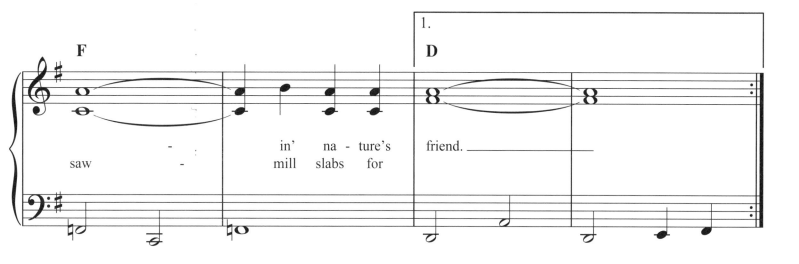

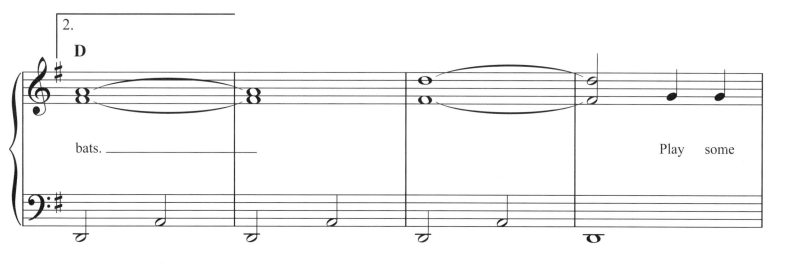

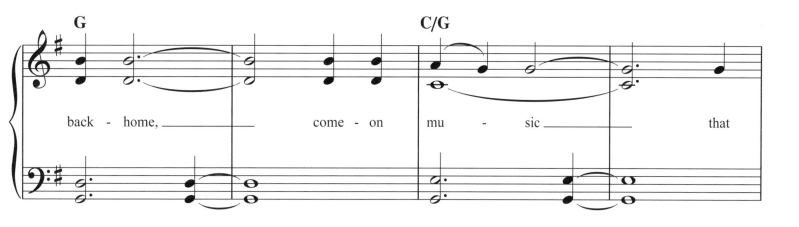

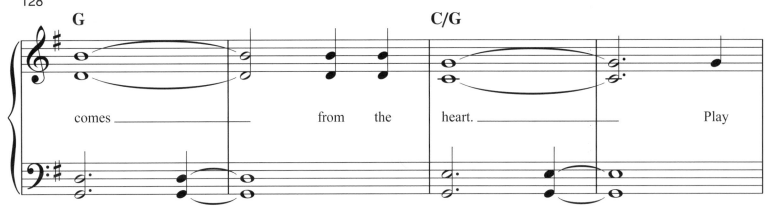

comes _____ from the heart. _____ Play

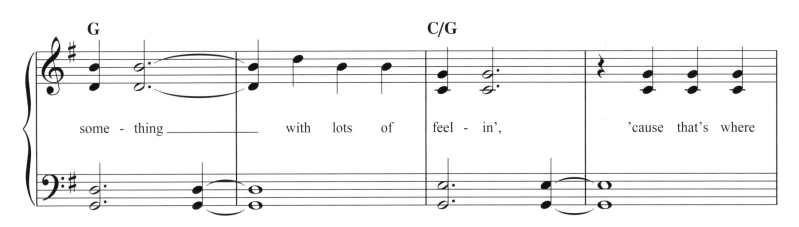

some - thing _____ with lots of feel - in', 'cause that's where

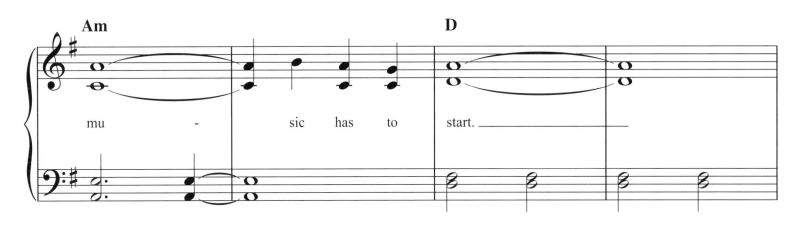

mu - sic has to start. _____

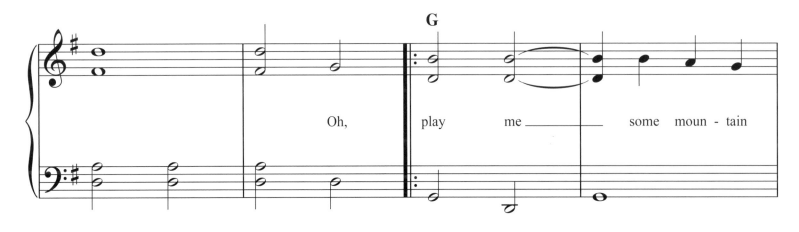

Oh, play me _____ some moun - tain

mu - sic, _____ like Grand - ma and Grand - pa used to

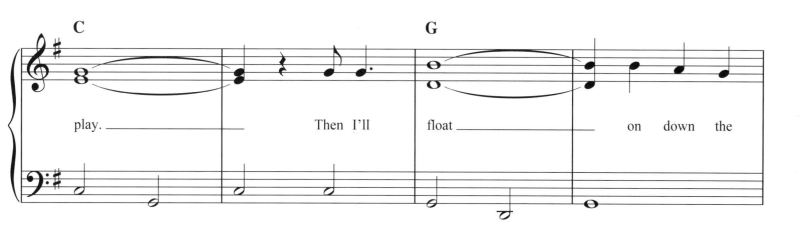

play. _____ Then I'll float _____ on down the

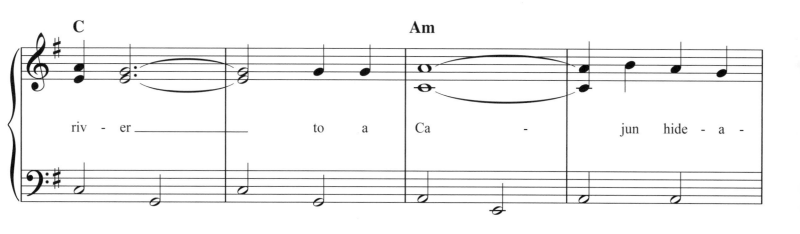

riv - er _____ to a Ca - jun hide - a -

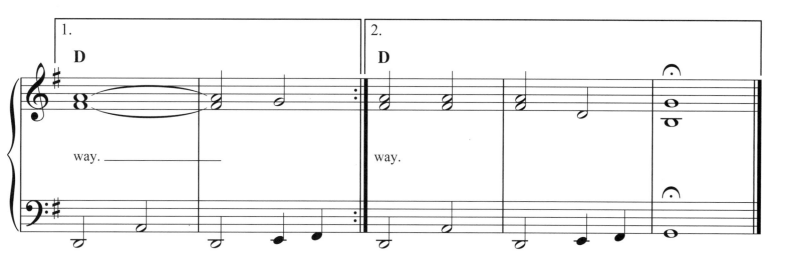

way. _____   way.

OH, LONESOME ME

Words and Music by
DON GIBSON

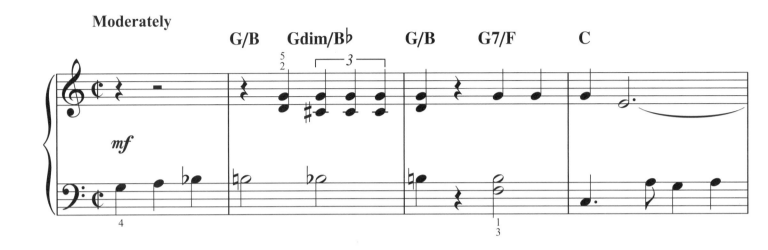

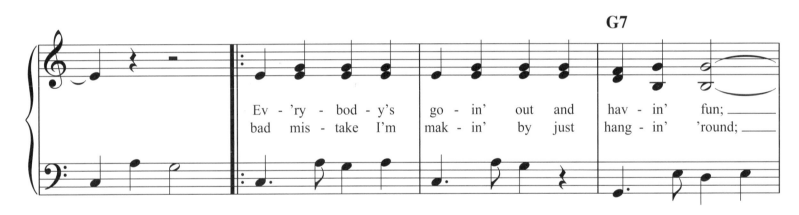

Ev - 'ry - bod - y's   go - in' out and   hav - in'   fun; ___
bad mis - take I'm   mak - in' by just   hang - in'   'round; ___

___   I'm   just a   fool for   stay - in'   home and
___   I   know that   I should   have some   fun and

hav - in' none. _____
paint the town. _____

I
A

can't get o - ver how she set me
love - sick fool that's blind and just can't

C   **C7**

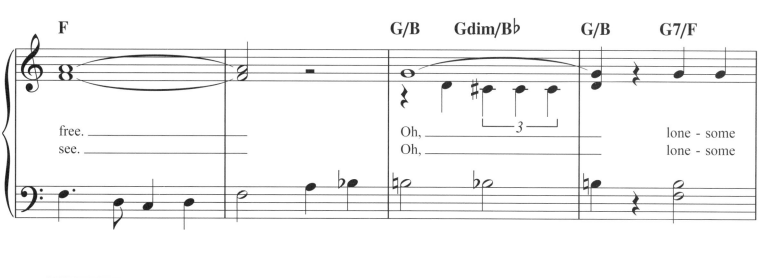

F   **G/B**   **Gdim/B♭**   **G/B**   **G7/F**

free. _____
see. _____

Oh, _____
Oh, _____

lone - some
lone - some

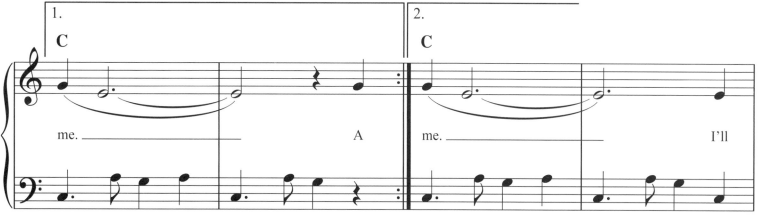

1.   2.

C   **C**

me. _____   A

me. _____   I'll

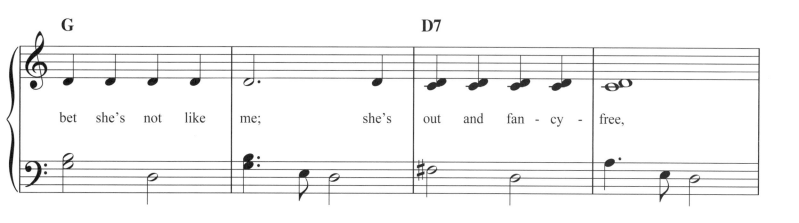

G   **D7**

bet she's not like me;   she's out and fan - cy - free,

flirt - ing with the boys with all her charms, _____ but

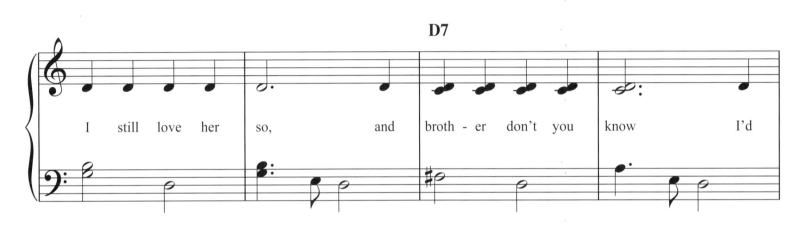

I still love her so, and broth - er don't you know I'd

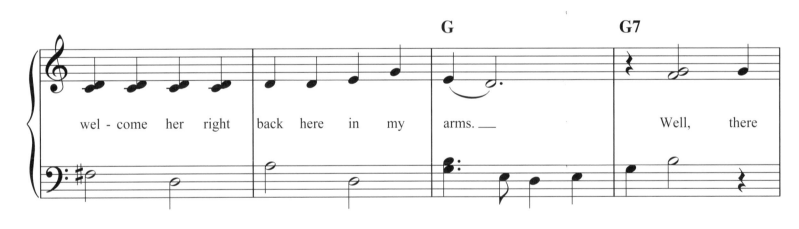

wel - come her right back here in my arms. __ Well, there

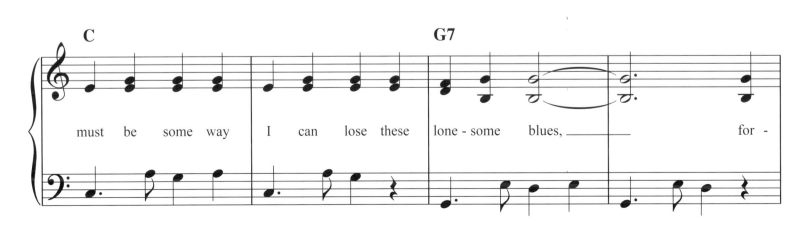

must be some way I can lose these lone - some blues, _____ for -

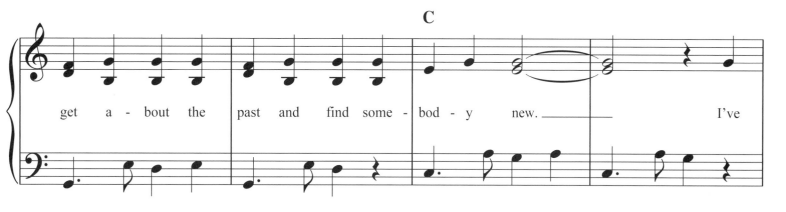

get a - bout the past and find some - bod - y new. _____ I've

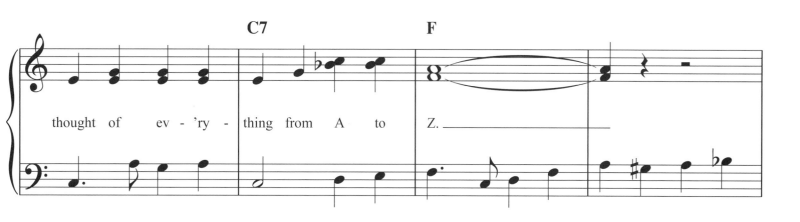

thought of ev - 'ry - thing from A to Z. _____

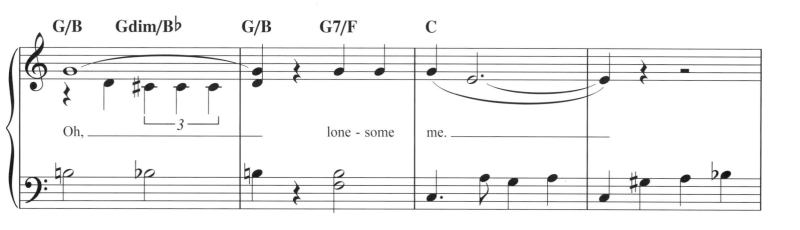

Oh, _____ lone - some me.

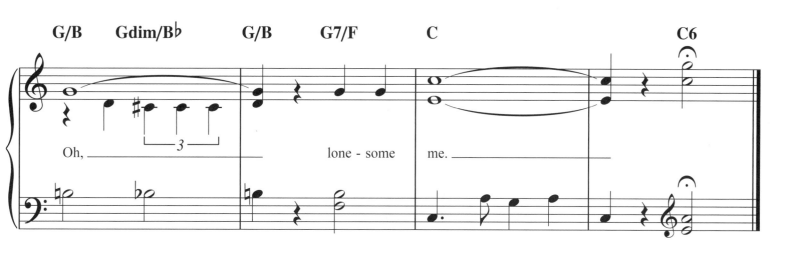

Oh, _____ lone - some me. _____

RELEASE ME

Words and Music by ROBERT YOUNT,
EDDIE MILLER and DUB WILLIAMS

Moderately slow

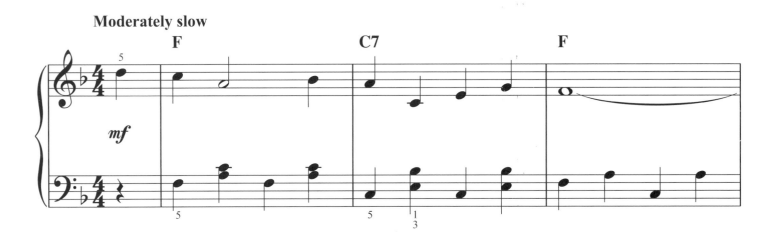

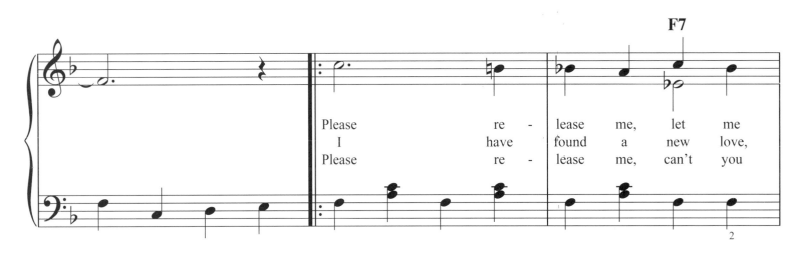

Please   re - lease me, let me
I   have found a new love,
Please   re - lease me, can't you

go, _____ for   I   don't
dear, _____ and   I   will
see _____ you'd   be   a

RING OF FIRE

Words and Music by MERLE KILGORE
and JUNE CARTER

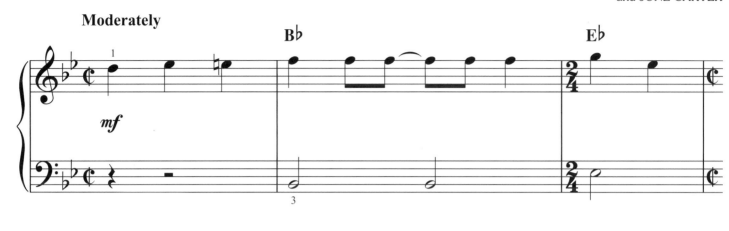

Love _____ is a burn-ing
taste _____ of __ love is

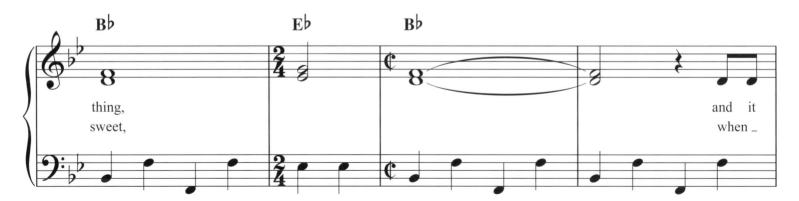

thing,   and it
sweet,   when _

makes _____ a fi - ery ring.
hearts _____ like ours ___ beat.

Bound _____ by wild de -
I fell for you like a

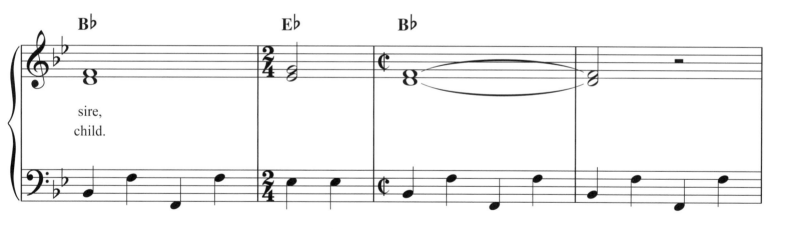

sire,
child.

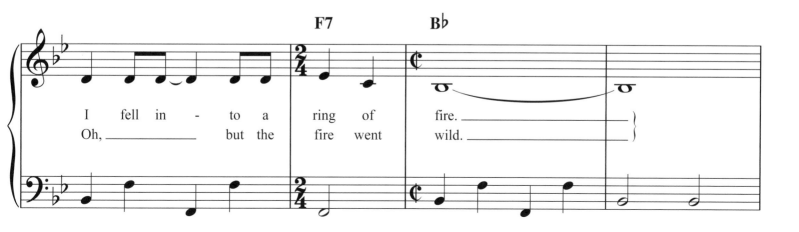

I fell in - to a ring of fire. _____
Oh, _____ but the fire went wild. _____

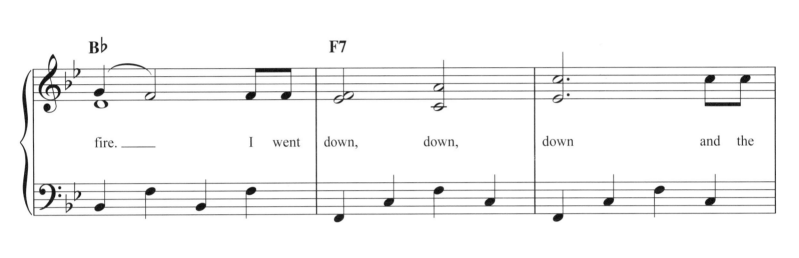

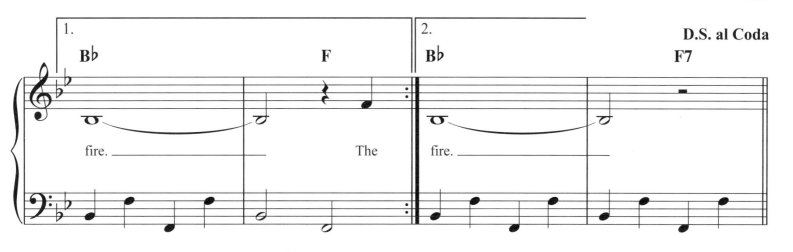

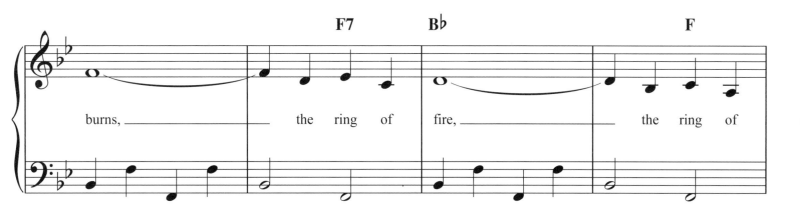

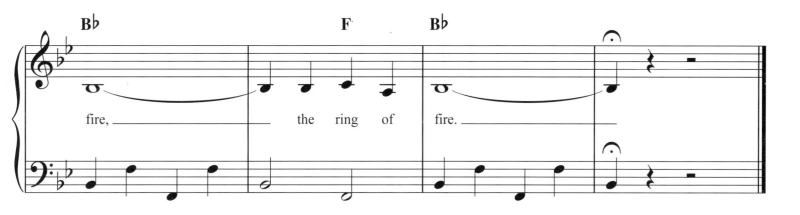

SAN ANTONIO ROSE

from SAN ANTONIO ROSE

By BOB WILLS

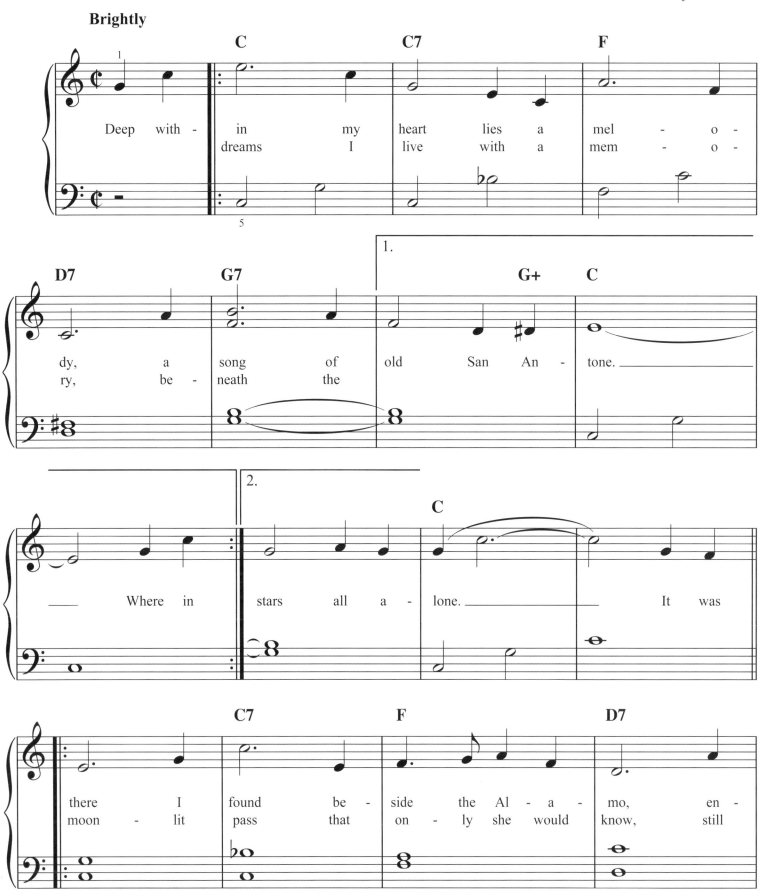

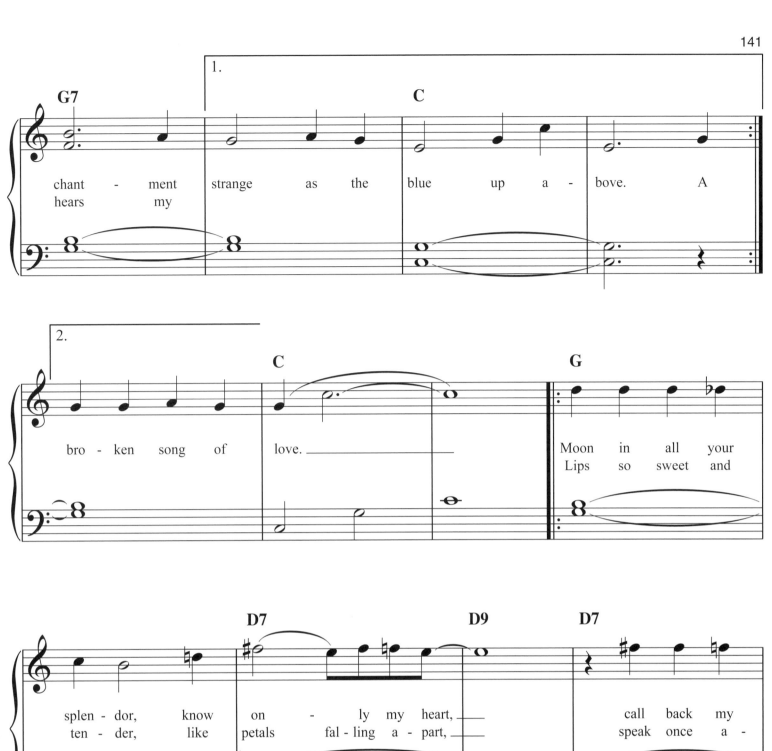

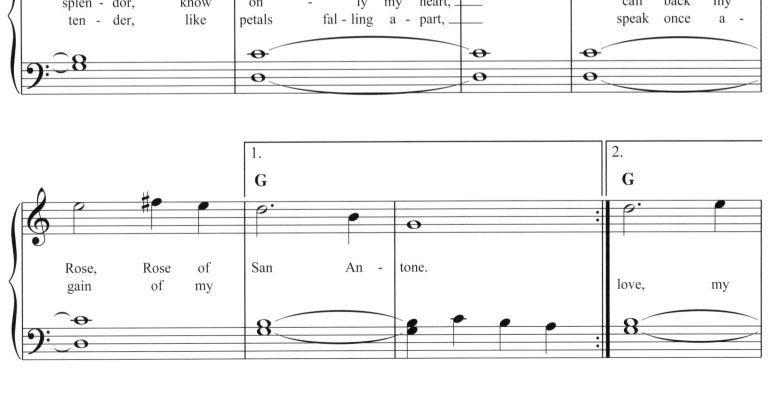

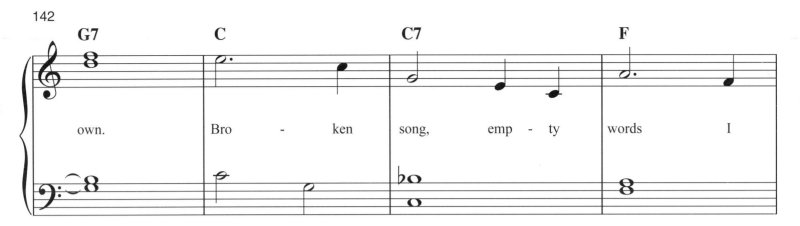

own. Bro - ken song, emp - ty words I

know still live in my heart all a - lone, ____

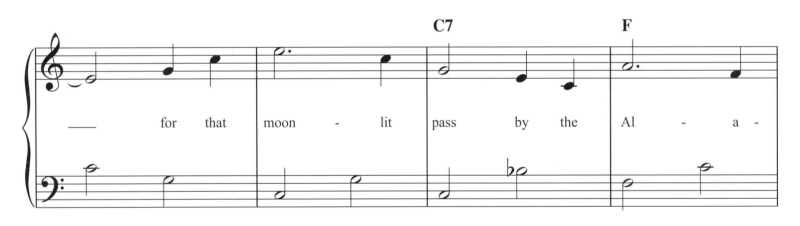

____ for that moon - lit pass by the Al - a -

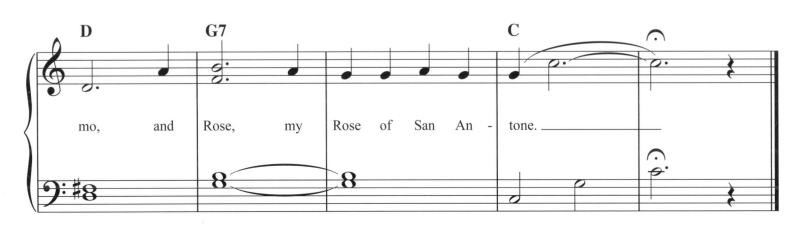

mo, and Rose, my Rose of San An - tone. ____

TENNESSEE WALTZ

Words and Music by REDD STEWART
and PEE WEE KING

Country Waltz

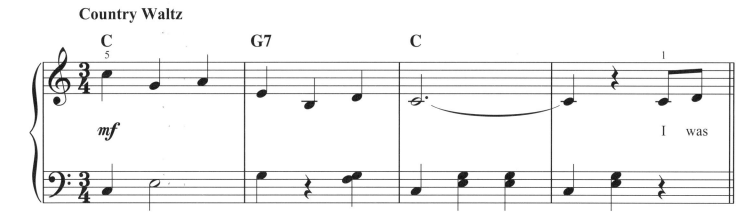

waltz-ing ___ with my dar-lin' ___ to the Ten-nes - see ___

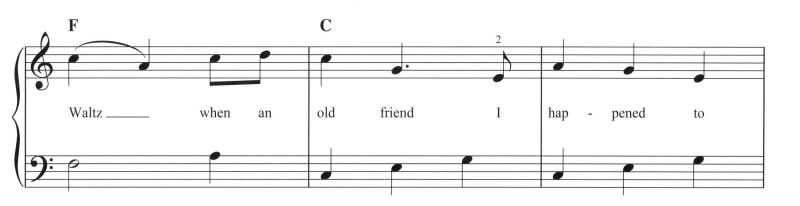

Waltz ___ when an old friend I hap-pened to

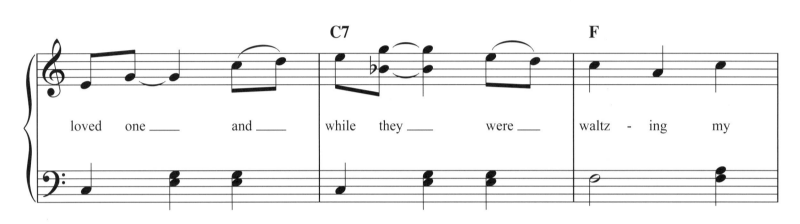

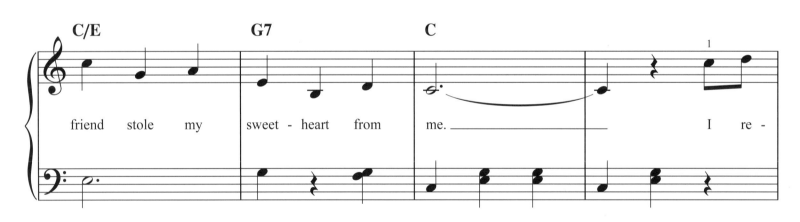

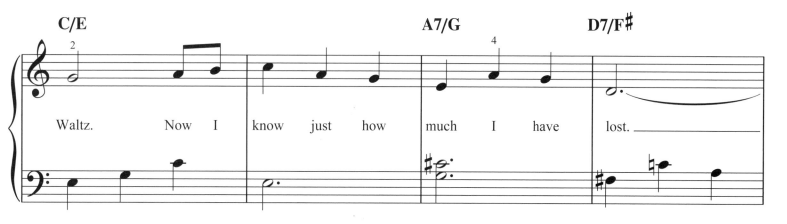

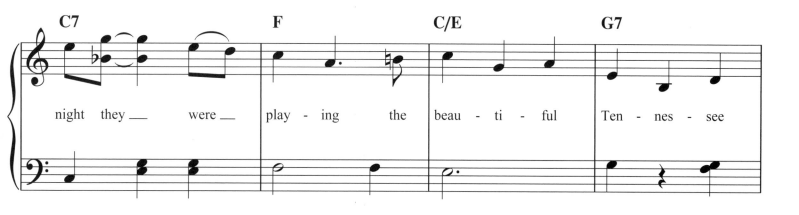

SMOKY MOUNTAIN RAIN

Words and Music by KYE FLEMING
and DENNIS MORGAN

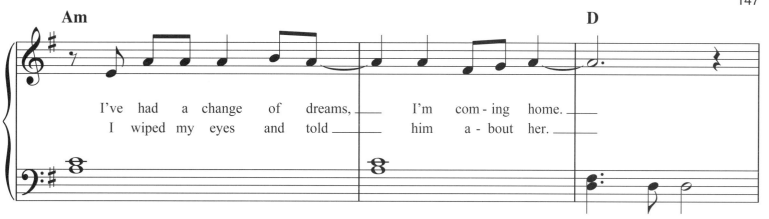

Am　　　　　　　　　　　　　　　　　　　　　　**D**

I've had a change of dreams, ____ I'm com - ing home. ____
I wiped my eyes and told ____ him a - bout her. ____

　　　　　　　　　　　　C

But tears filled my eyes ____ when I found out she was gone. ____
I've got to find her, ____ can't you make these big wheels burn? ____

D　　　　　　　　　　　　**C**　**D**　**G**

Smok - y Moun - tain rain ____

Bm　　　　　　　　　　　　　　　　**C**

____ keeps on fall - ing, I keep on call - ing ____

her name. ___ Smok - y Moun - tain rain, ___

___ I'll keep on search - ing; I can't go on hurt - ing ___

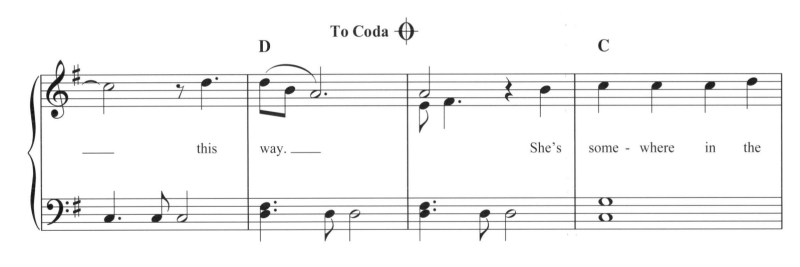

To Coda

___ this way. ___ She's some - where in the

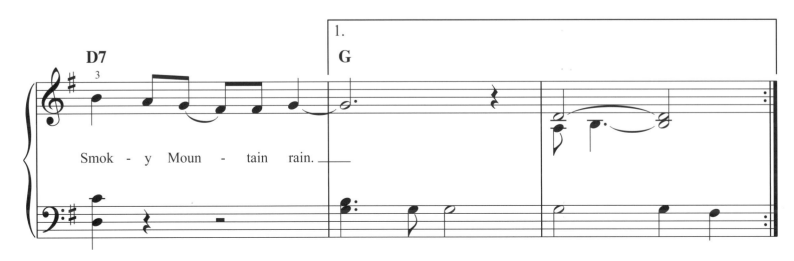

Smok - y Moun - tain rain. ___

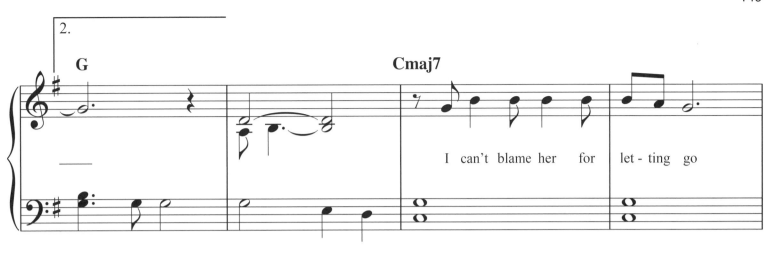

I can't blame her for let - ting go

a wom - an needs some - one warm __ to hold. __ I feel the rain run - ning

down __ my face; __ I'll find her no mat - ter what __ it takes.

D.S. al Coda

CODA

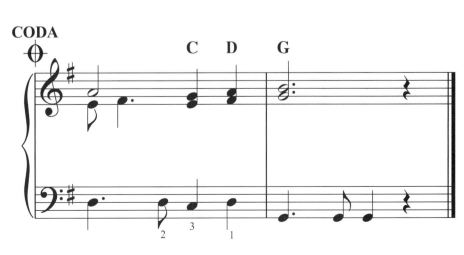

STAND BY YOUR MAN

Words and Music by TAMMY WYNETTE
and BILLY SHERRILL

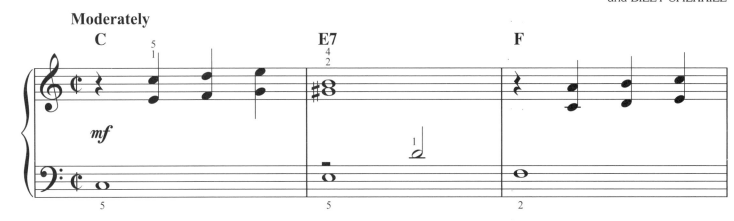

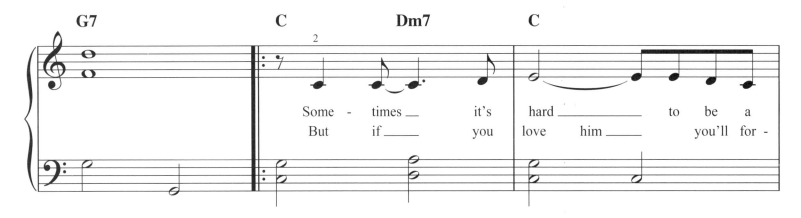

Some - times _____ it's hard _____ to be a
But if _____ you love him _____ you'll for -

wom - an, _____ giv - ing all your
give him, _____ e - ven though he's

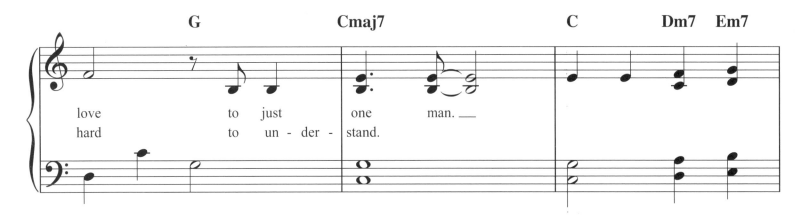

love to just one man. _____
hard to un - der - stand.

Fmaj7 · · · F6 · F · G · **1.** Cmaj7

You'll have ___ bad times and he'll have
And if you love him,

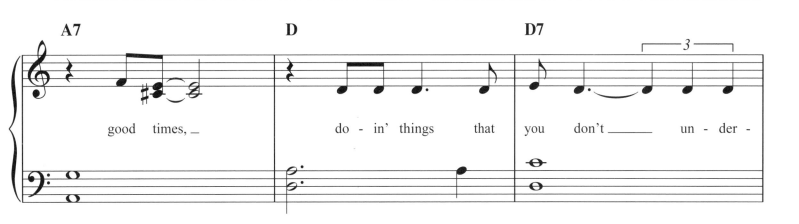

A7 · D · D7

good times, ___ do - in' things that you don't _____ un - der -

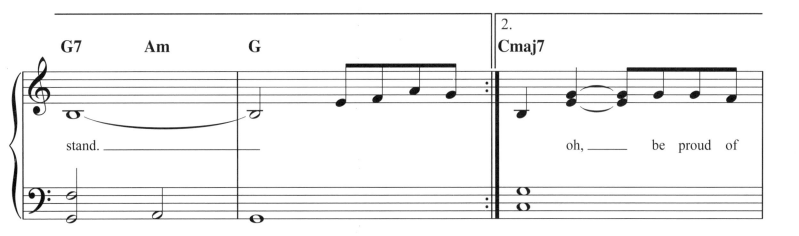

G7 · Am · G · **2.** Cmaj7

stand. _____ oh, _____ be proud of

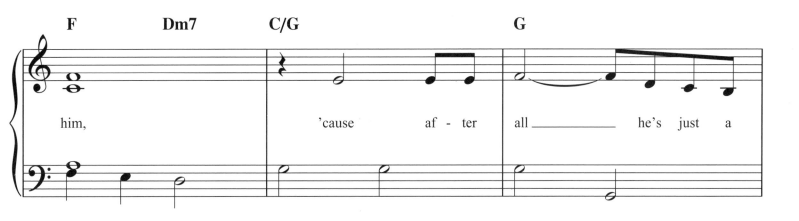

F · Dm7 · C/G · G

him, 'cause af - ter all _____ he's just a

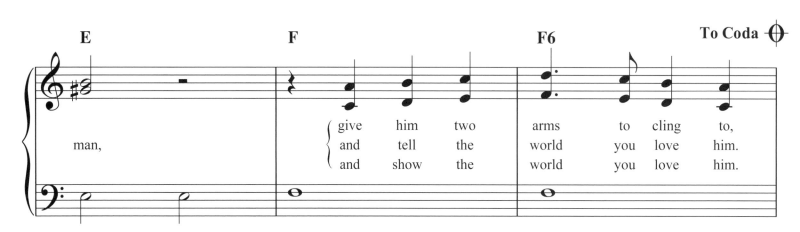

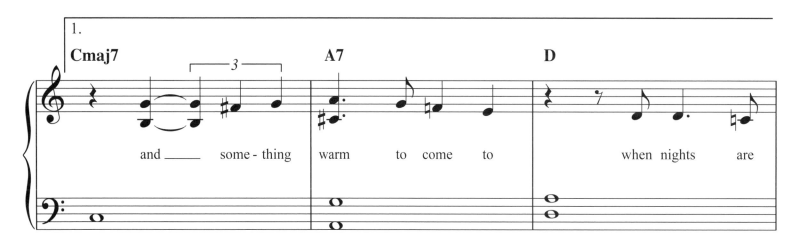

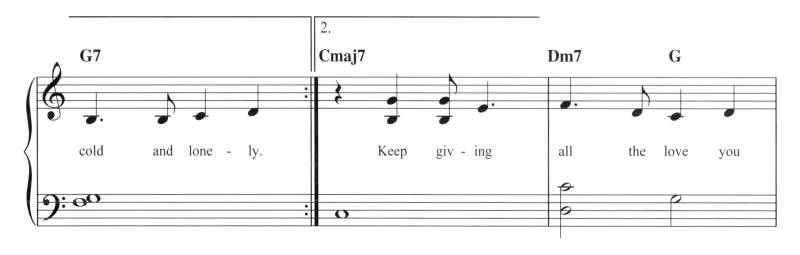

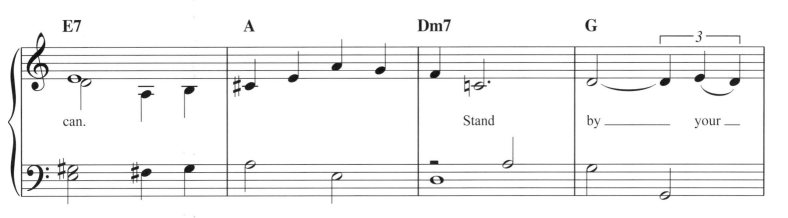

can.

Stand

by _____ your _____

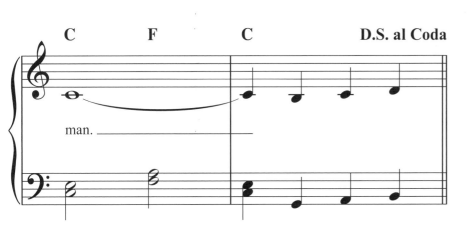

man. _____

D.S. al Coda

CODA

Keep giv - ing

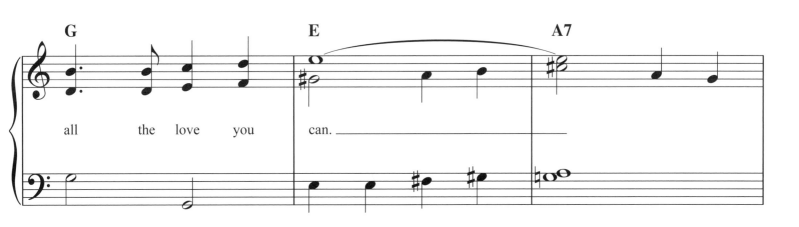

all the love you can. _____

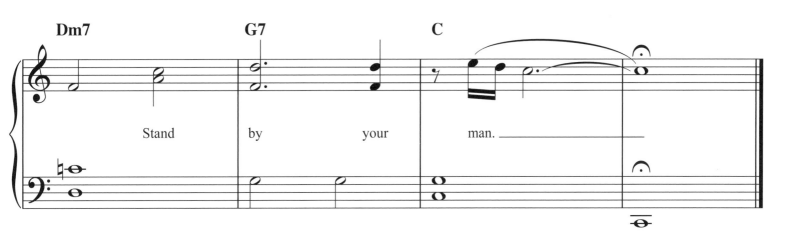

Stand by your man. _____

WALKIN' AFTER MIDNIGHT

Lyrics by DON HECHT
Music by ALAN W. BLOCK

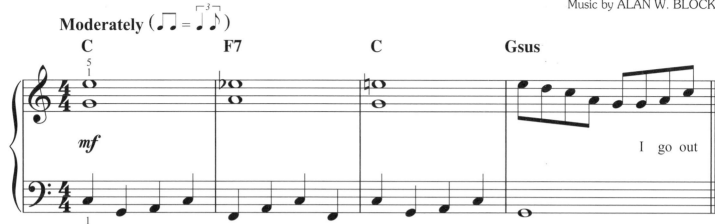

walk-in' _____ af - ter mid - night _____ in _____ the moon - light _____ just

like we used to do. I'm al - ways walk-in' _____ af - ter mid-night search - in' for

you. _____ I walk for miles _____ a - long the

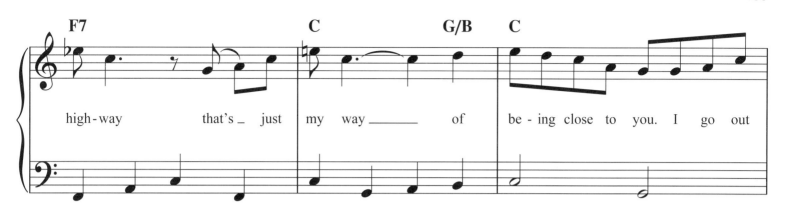

high-way that's _ just my way _____ of be - ing close to you. I go out

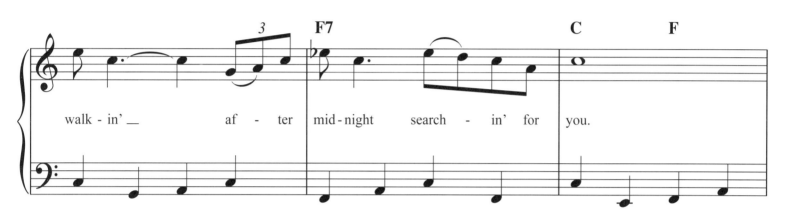

walk - in' _ af - ter mid - night search - in' for you.

I stop to see a weep - in' wil - low cry - in' on his pil - low,

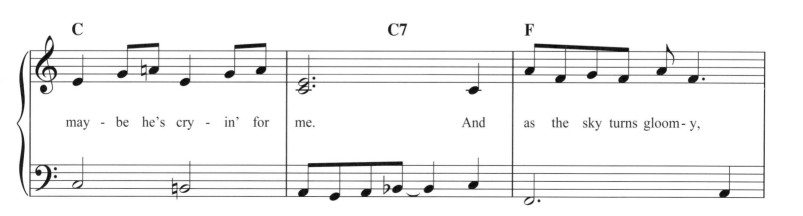

may - be he's cry - in' for me. And as the sky turns gloom - y,

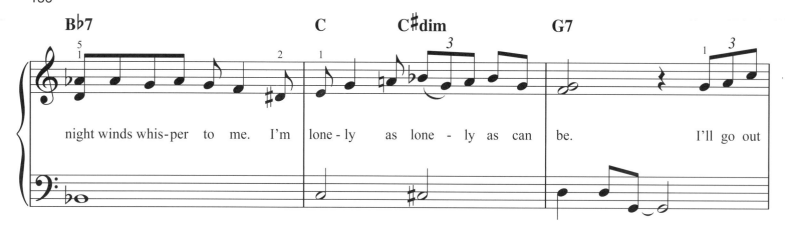

Bb7 · **C** · **C#dim** · **G7**

night winds whis-per to me. I'm lone - ly as lone - ly as can be. I'll go out

C · **F7** · **C** · **G/B**

walk - in' _____ af - ter mid - night _____ in ___ the star - light _____ and

C · **F7**

pray that you may be some-where just walk - in' _____ af - ter mid-night search - in' for

1.
C **F** **C**

me. _____ I go out

2.
C **F** **C**

me.

WALKING THE FLOOR OVER YOU

Words and Music by
ERNEST TUBB

Bright Texas Swing

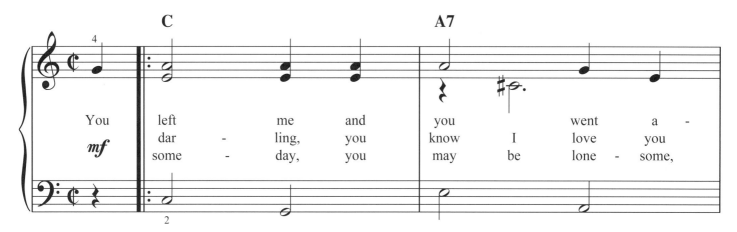

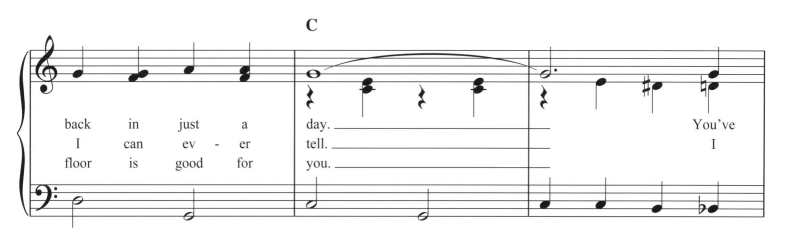

158

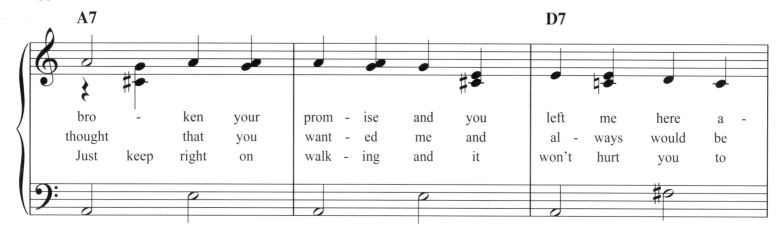

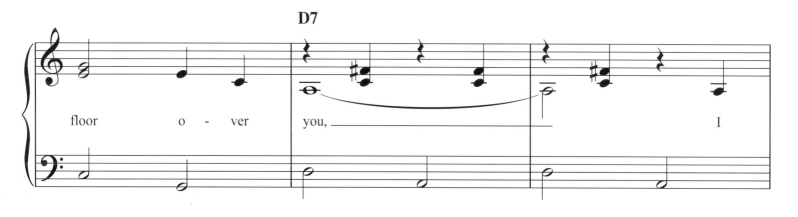

can't sleep a wink, that is true. _____

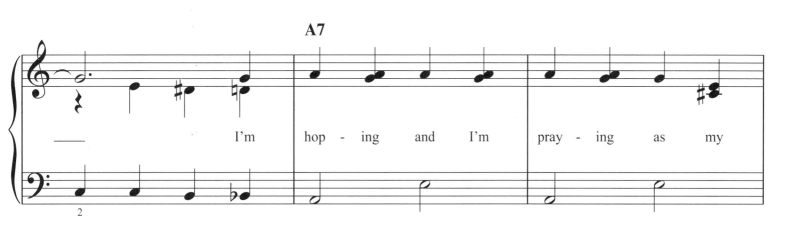

_____ I'm hop - ing and I'm pray - ing as my

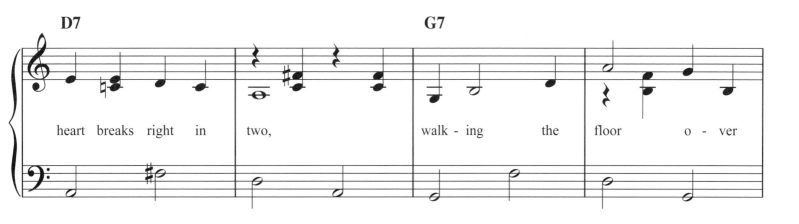

heart breaks right in two, walk - ing the floor o - ver

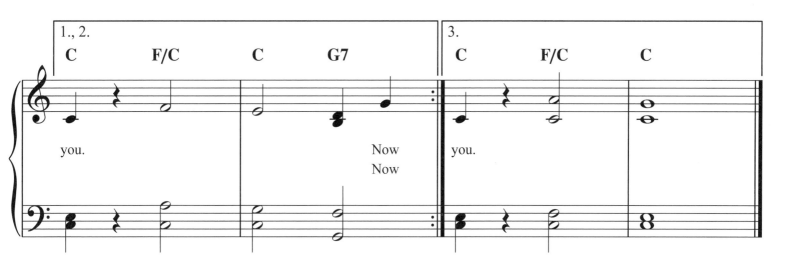

you.

Now
Now

you.

WELCOME TO MY WORLD

Words and Music by RAY WINKLER
and JOHN HATHCOCK

Moderately

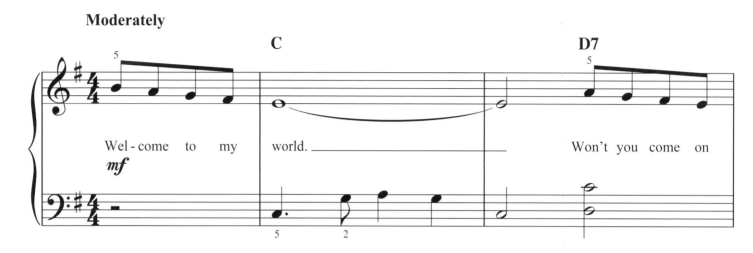

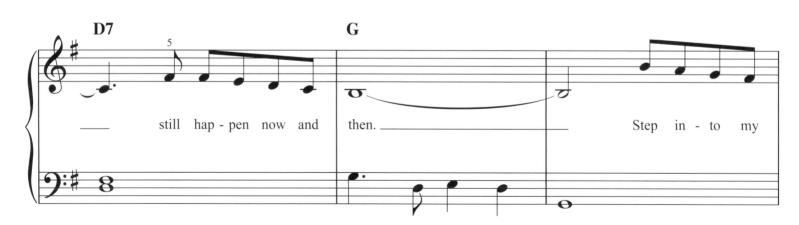

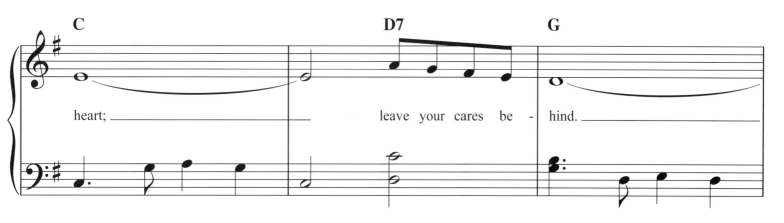

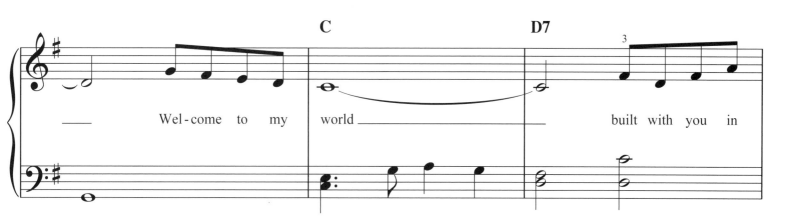

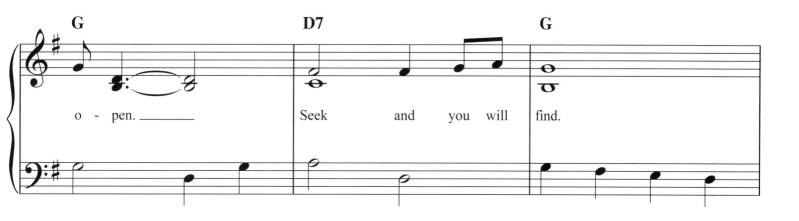

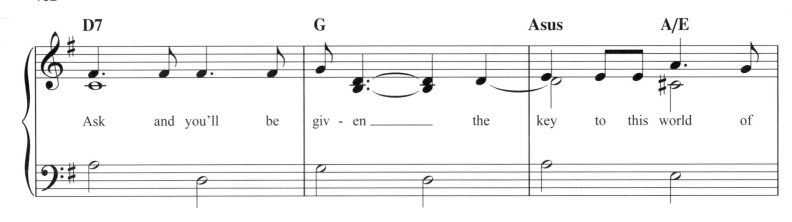

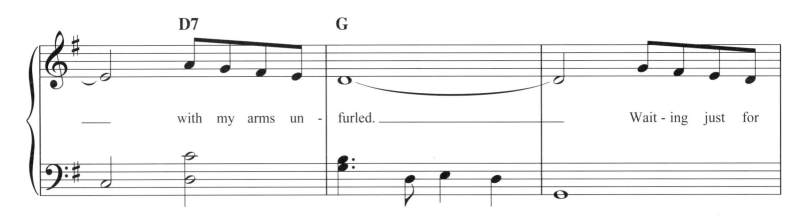

WICHITA LINEMAN

Words and Music by
JIMMY WEBB

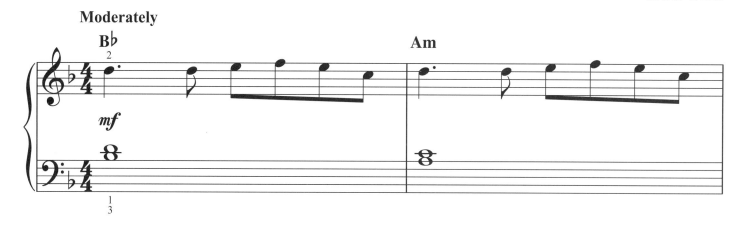

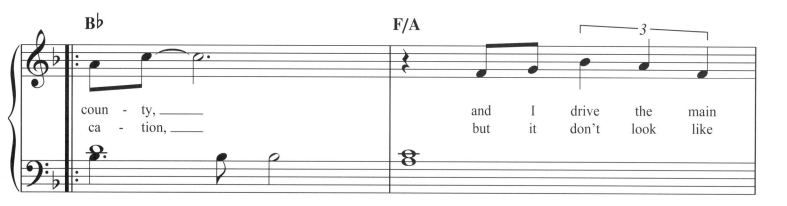

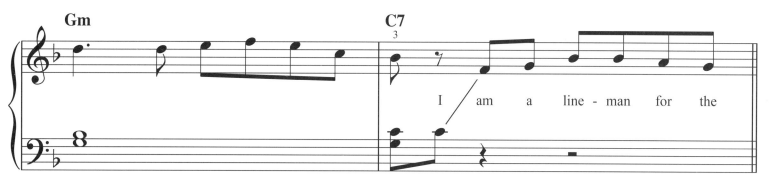

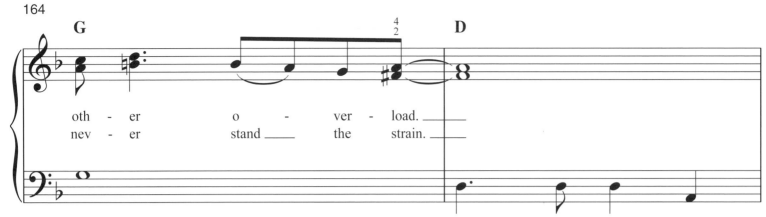

oth - er o - ver - load. _____
nev - er stand _____ the strain. _____

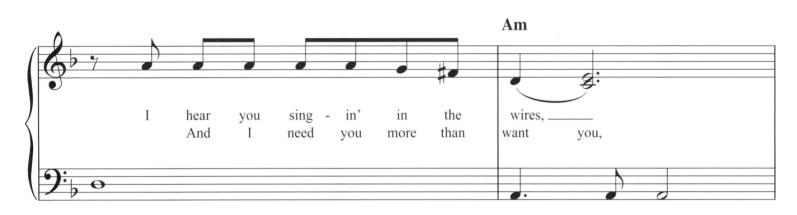

I hear you sing - in' in the wires, _____
And I need you more than want you,

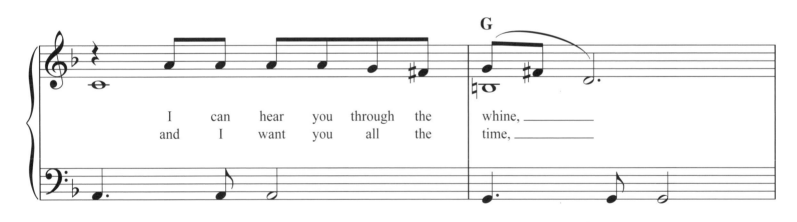

I can hear you through the whine, _____
and I want you all the time, _____

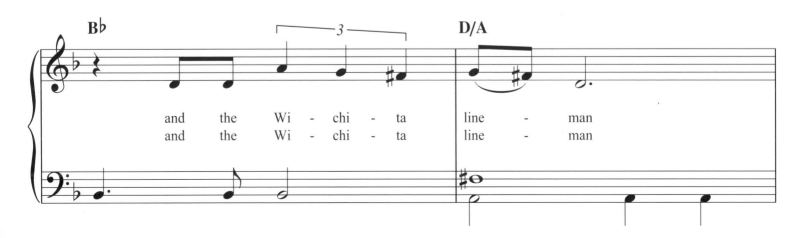

and the Wi - chi - ta line - man
and the Wi - chi - ta line - man

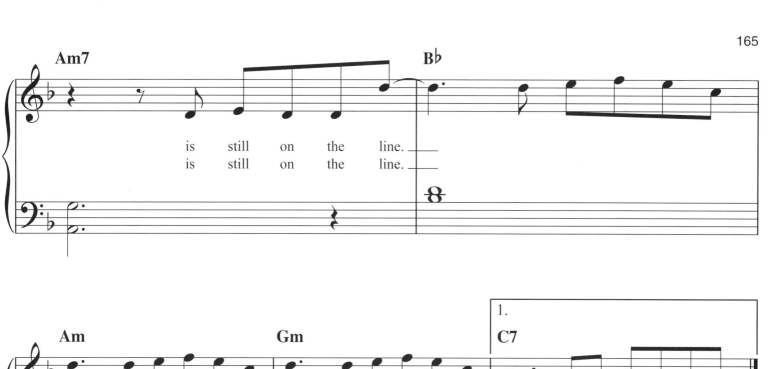

is   still   on   the   line. ____
is   still   on   the   line. ____

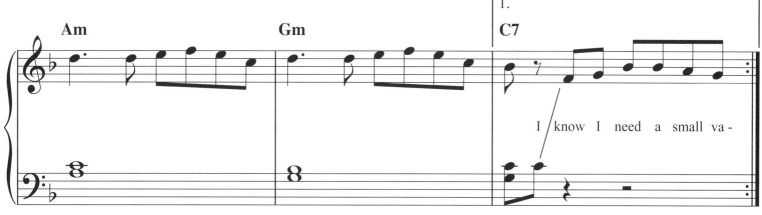

1.

I / know I need a small va -

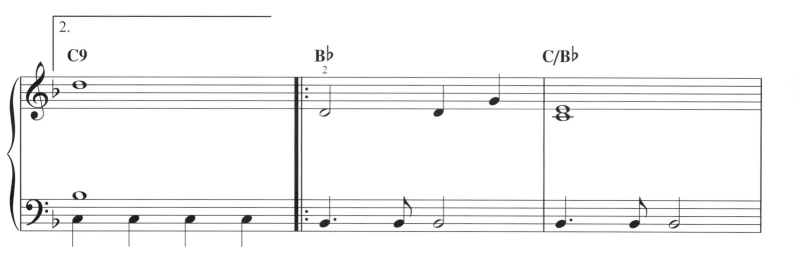

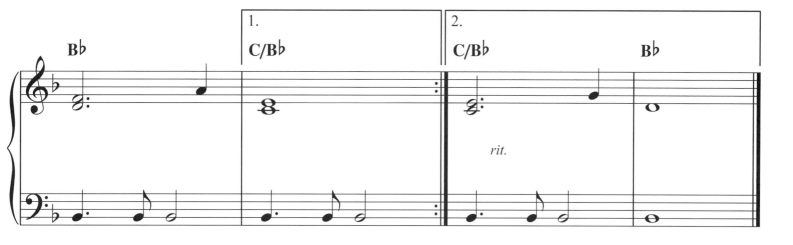

rit.

YOU ARE MY SUNSHINE

Words and Music by
JIMMIE DAVIS

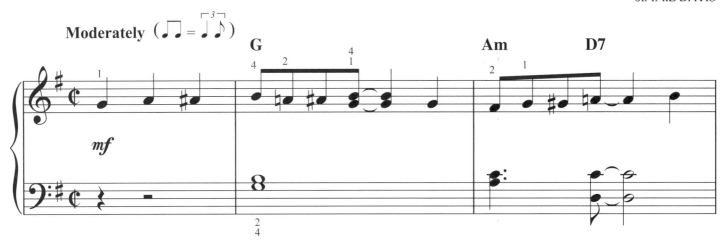

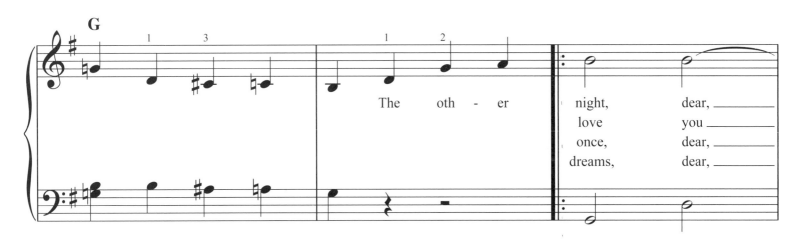

The oth-er night, dear, _____
love you _____
once, dear, _____
dreams, dear, _____

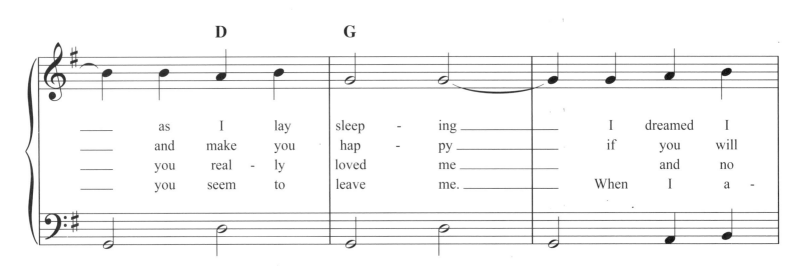

_____ as I lay sleep - ing _____ I dreamed I
_____ and make you hap - py _____ if you will
_____ you real - ly loved me _____ and no
_____ you seem to leave me. _____ When I a -

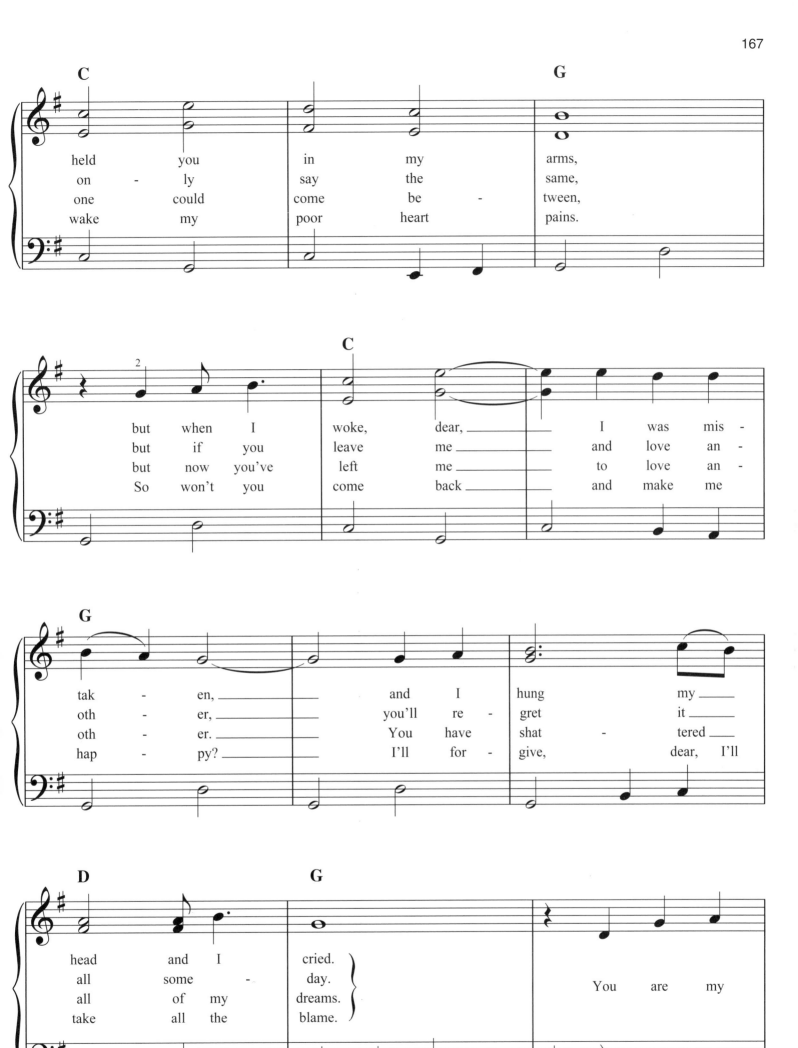

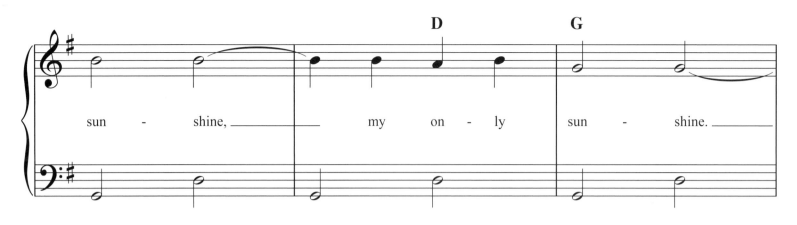

sun - shine, _____ my on - ly sun - shine. _____

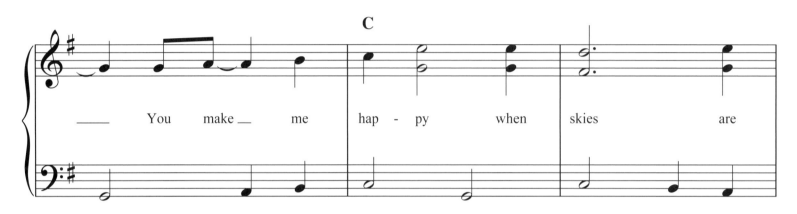

_____ You make ___ me hap - py when skies are

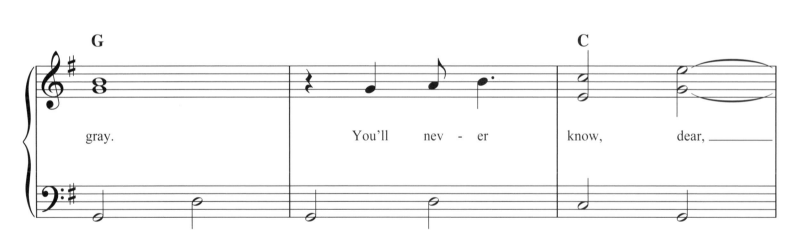

gray. You'll nev - er know, dear, _____

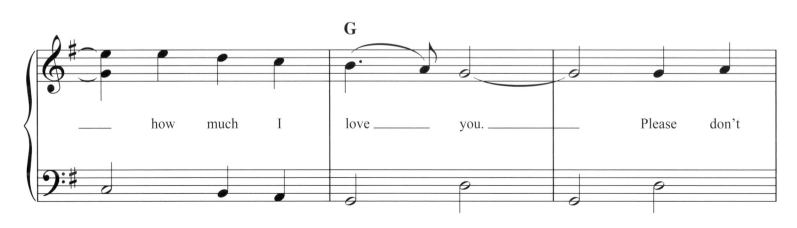

_____ how much I love _____ you. _____ Please don't

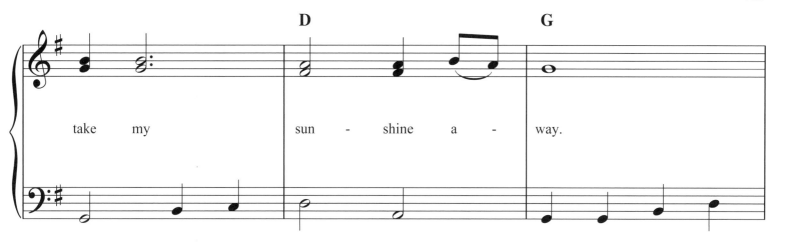

take my   sun - shine   a -   way.

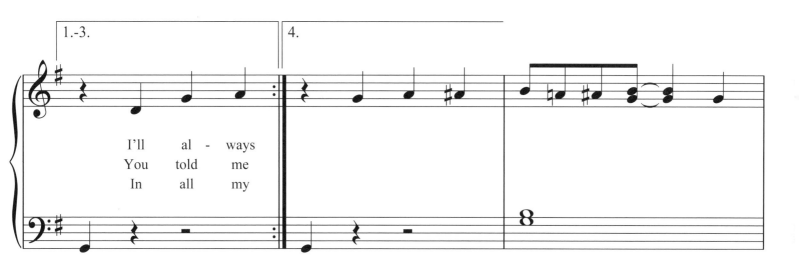

I'll   al -   ways
You   told   me
In   all   my

YOU DON'T KNOW ME

Words and Music by CINDY WALKER
and EDDY ARNOLD

Slow Swing Ballad

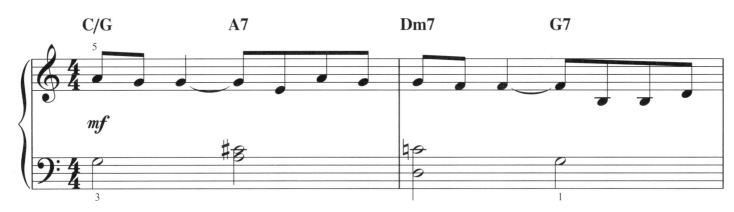

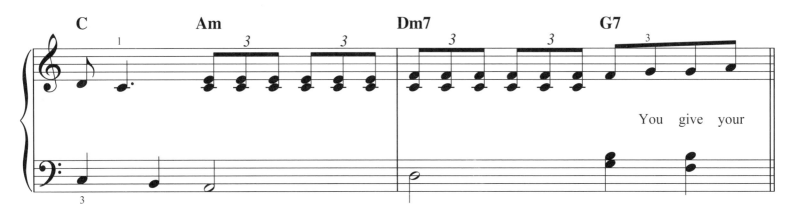

You give your

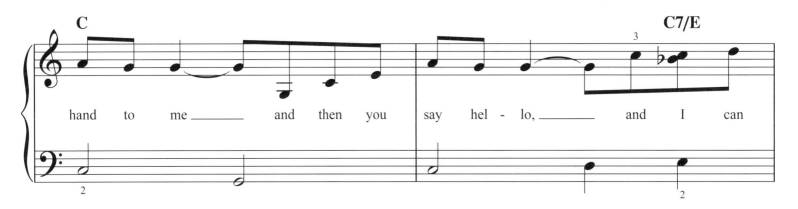

hand to me _____ and then you say hel - lo, _____ and I can

hard - ly speak, _____ my heart is beat - ing so. _____ And an - y-

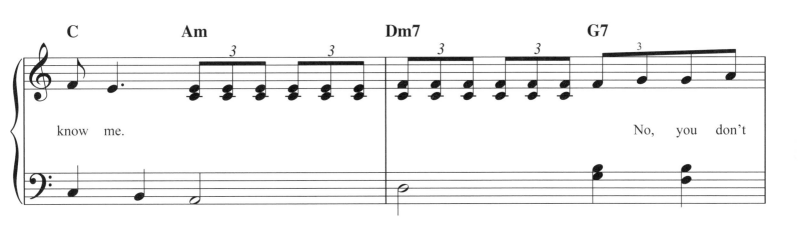

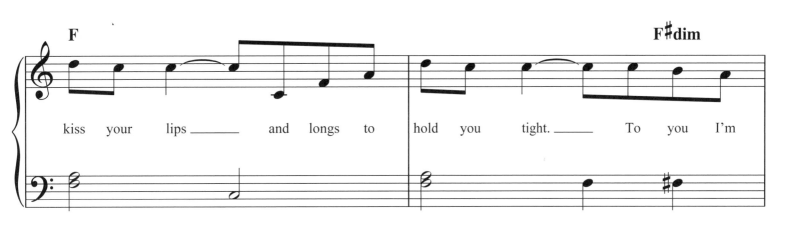

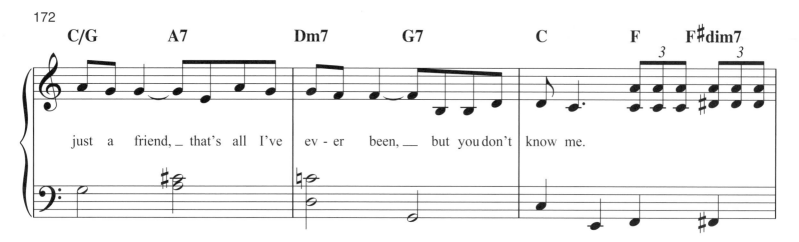

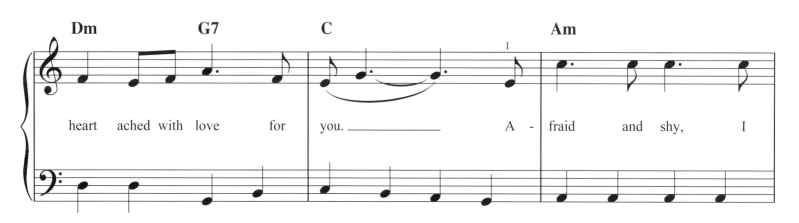

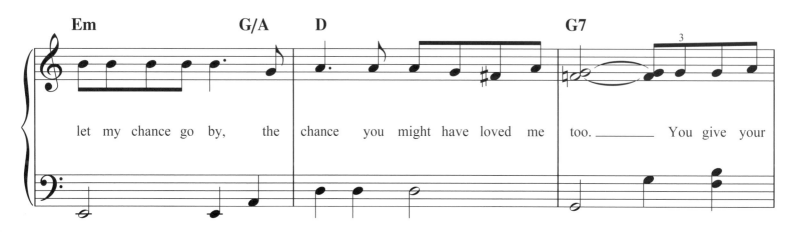

C · · · · · · · · · · **C7/E**

hand to me _____ and then you say good - bye. _____ I watch you

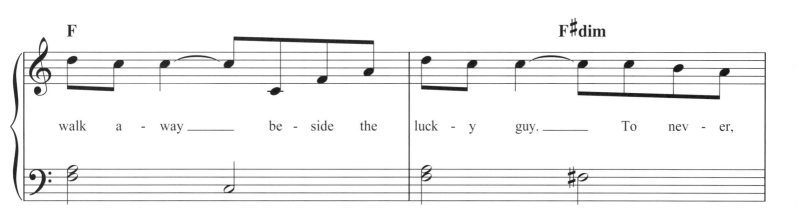

F · · · · · · · · · · **F♯dim**

walk a - way _____ be - side the luck - y guy. _____ To nev - er,

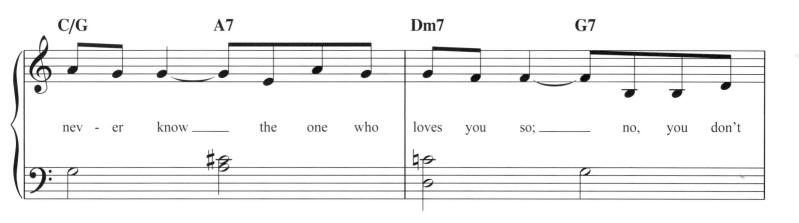

C/G · · **A7** · · · **Dm7** · · **G7**

nev - er know _____ the one who loves you so; _____ no, you don't

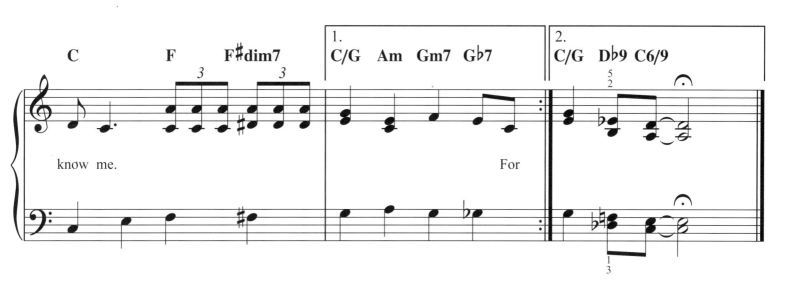

C · · **F** · **F♯dim7** · · **1.** **C/G Am Gm7 G♭7** · · **2.** **C/G D♭9 C6/9**

know me. · · · · · · · · · For

YOUR CHEATIN' HEART

Words and Music by
HANK WILLIAMS

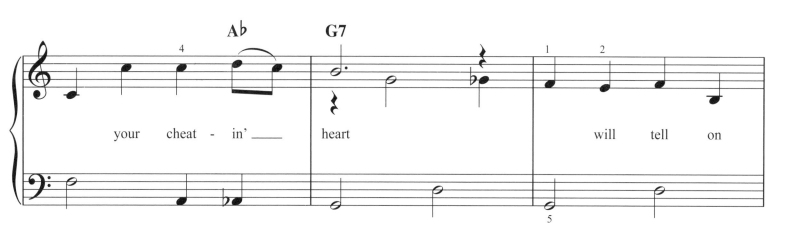

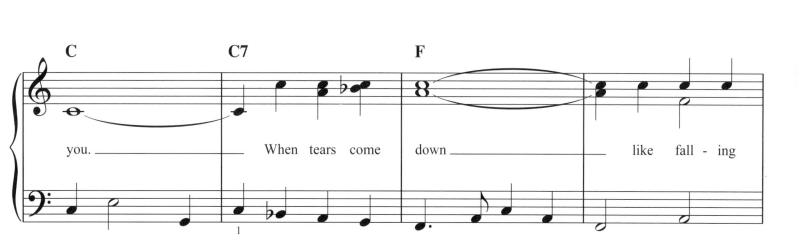

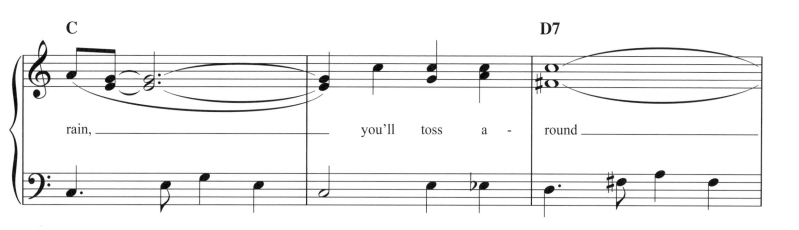

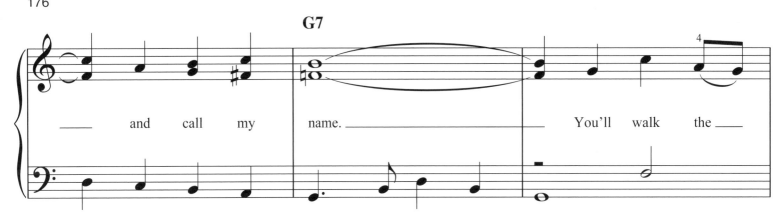

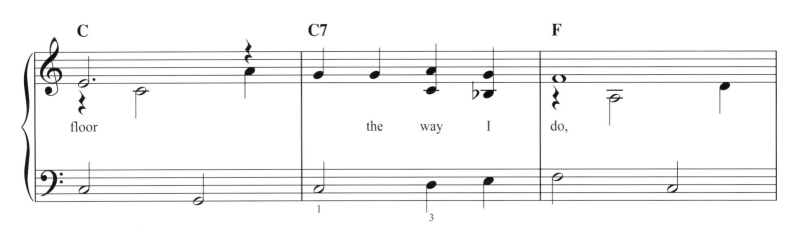

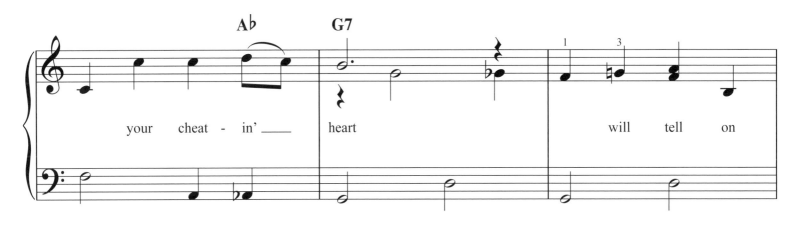

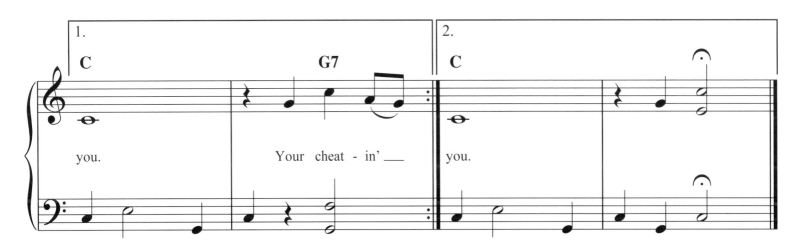